Steve

You have given me your Casa Sirena + Isla Mujeres - in return I give you 'my Italy'

Love,
Charlotte

la **dolce**
*the sweet*
*life*
# Vita

Happy Birthday!
2008

# la dolce vita

*the sweet life*

## IN CORTONA, TUSCANY ITALY

CHARLOTTE PHILLIPS

TATE PUBLISHING & Enterprises

TATE PUBLISHING
& *Enterprises*

Book design copyright © 2006 by Tate Publishing, LLC. All rights reserved.
*Cover design by Taylor Rauschkolb*
*Interiror design by Janae Glass*

*Published in the United States of America*

ISBN: 1-5988661-9-2
06.09.07

# Contents

# Acknowledgments

To my darling children; Dennis, Carrie and Christy who taught me to 'be my best' and loved me when I was not. To my ex-husband and my mother for letting me fly. To my friend Jennie Ryland for the beautiful watercolor, the background for my book cover. To Stacy Baker at Tate Publishing. Thanks to my editor Kyle Swanson and my graphic designers Taylor Rausckolb and Janae Glass. To Amy and Giovanni, my family away from home. Many thanks to Sue and Avalon. To my dear friend Quay for always making me go the extra mile and walking that mile with me. To Kathy for reading my every word as fast as I could write them. To Angiolo for making my life in Cortona so great. To Molly for your hopes, dreams and prayers for me. And my profound thanks to all of the good people in my book.

This book is dedicated to my grandparents, my mother, my father and my brother . . . I am only very sorry you are not here to enjoy this with me. But you are always in my heart.

# My Perfect Life

I live in the most beautiful house in a very exclusive gated community. I love our house.

We have been here for almost two years, just enough time for me to have decorated perfectly and received all of the compliments from friends and family. I believe my life to be perfect with this perfect home, perfect grown children and the perfect husband. If I no longer lust for my husband, I do love him. He is my friend, my lover, my rock.

Our kitchen is European and commercial for all our dinner parties. We love to entertain with the special meals I prepare. Kevin and I travel extensively and I have collected cookbooks from restaurants all over the world. I have hundreds of them and I have cooked at least one thing from every cookbook.

Kevin is about to retire and I retired two years ago. Before my retirement, we lived a very complicated but fun life. I lived and worked in California and our home, where Kevin resided was in Plano, Texas. Kevin travels for business almost weekly and was not home often. We would meet on weekends in New York City, Chicago, Boston, D.C., Vegas, San Francisco or some other fun place. Or we would hook up at an airport and fly to Europe for as many days as either of us could manage. Life was great and we loved it, even though it was hectic.

When I retired and returned from California, we bought our dream home with its vast front porch overlooking the lake, its beautifully manicured yard, pool with jacuzzi and 6,000 sq. ft. for us to roam and play. Kevin had his media room and I had my art room. Could life get better?

It was early evening and I was preparing dinner, waiting for Kevin to return home from a business trip. The wine was chilled and appetizers waiting. When he walked in, I was all smiles, about to cross the room for a welcome home hug and kiss, when I noticed he had a very serious, almost dangerous look on his face. I stopped in my tracks, imagining a bad accident or worse, and asked, "What is wrong?"

Maintaining that ever so serious look he simply stated, "I want a divorce. I've thought about it and there is no point in discussing anything other than a settlement."

I couldn't move, I couldn't breathe. He walked off through the study into the master bedroom without saying another word. I poured a glass of wine and went to the back patio. I sat there overlooking the pool, not seeing, not feeling, just sitting there. I could not make sense of any of this so I just sat, it felt like for hours.

At some point Kevin came to the back door and said he was going to a hotel and would e-mail me later. I looked down and saw two suitcases and then he was gone. I sat on my patio for hours; I only moved to retrieve the bottle of wine.

My thoughts were all over the page not comprehending what had happened, what had possibly changed and how my once perfect world had just come crashing down. After days of sitting, not answering the phone, not checking e-mails, I finally decided to call my friend Quay. When she answered the phone I was crying, ranting and raving.

She said, "Don't move. I am on my way."

I am sure she thought I had gone absolutely mad. My conversation, my words were garbled and unintelligible.

Quay arrived, my tears dried, I said, "Quay, I need to move and I want to move today."

I knew of some new town homes being built in Frisco so that is where we started looking and where we finished looking. I bought the first one I looked at and moved in nineteen days.

My town home was almost complete when I contracted for it. I made some changes, painted the kitchen Chinese red, the living room burnt umber and put in the backyard, the patio and the gas grille.

I woke up many months later in a strange bed, in a strange place and wondered where in the world I was and what in the world had happened. It then dawned on me, that now I was divorced and living in a new place. Just me and my dog Jake. Jake was lying beside me on the bed. I looked at him and thought, *Jake you need a Lucy to keep you company.* So Jake, my 2-year-old dog and I went dog shopping. We found his

Lucy, a beautiful Japanese Chin, black and white with the sweetest face in the world. We became three.

Kevin called not long after Lucy, Jake and I became a family and said he needed to meet with me and tell me some things. *Okay, I can do that, when and where?* We met for lunch the next day. He looked great. He had lost weight, was sporting a new look and driving a new BMW 720. I looked across the table at him and thought, *I don't miss you any more. I like my new life.*

It's good I had those thoughts spinning in my head because what he needed to talk to me about came as a real shock. He was dating a special woman, and was very attracted to her, and had in fact asked her to marry him. They were getting married in two weeks. Wow, life does change and we do move on. Some of us at record speeds. It seemed like just last week he told me he did not want to be married. I said as much to him and about the time it came out of my mouth, I realized he wanted to be married, just not to me. I congratulated him, declined lunch and left.

I went home and booked a flight to Paris, leaving the next day. I boarded the dogs, left town and decided I would not come back until after his nuptials. I did not want to read about it in the papers, or hear about it from friends. When I got to Paris, I rented a car and just started driving the country side.

After a week I found myself in Cortona, Italy, the heart of Tuscany. I fell in love with the town and the people. I started dreaming of living there. I knew it could only be a dream as I had grown children, grandchildren and an aging mother at home. But dreams are safe like that and you can just keep dreaming. I drove back to Paris after a couple of weeks and flew back home.

Sure enough, upon my return I heard all about the wedding, the honeymoon, the very large ring and the new multi-million dollar home. The only real feelings I had were thse of losing my best friend. It is now September and I am starting a new life. I congratulate myself!

# Life with a View

My mother passed away. We had been on a family vacation with all of the kids and grandkids. After returning, mom and I started going to the casino every week. We both loved gambling. We usually lost, would complain about it all the way home but always returned the following week. Mom was a hoot when she would win. Usually a tight women, she would go wild with the tips and always insisted on buying dinner. We celebrated her 87 birthday in Vegas, just the two of us. It was great fun!

Soon after mom's birthday, two of my children, a son-in-law and I went to Cancun for a short four-day vacation. Mom didn't want to go and decided to stay home and take care of Jake and Lucy. She loved those dogs and they loved her. When we returned home I went to mom's to collect the dogs. She said that she was feeling run down and had made a doctor's appointment for the next day. I asked her if she wanted me to take her and she said no, she felt like driving. I wasn't very concerned about mom's health. She was, after all, 87 and had always enjoyed good health. The doctor told her she appeared fine, gave her some iron pills and sent her home. One week later, she was in the hospital dying of pancreatic cancer. A week and a half later, she was gone. Life changes in a heartbeat. Now it's December, with Christmas just ahead and we should all be out shopping. All of us are still so stunned over mom's death that we just can't get in the mood. We know we have to for all of the kids, but it is hard and we remain reluctant.

With my children now grown and in their own homes, I am no longer the one carrying the sole responsibility for the dinners and parties. I think I feel relief, but at times I wish it was all like it used to be. I am not good to have too much time on my hands and I tend to get into trouble.

I woke up at two a.m. on December 23, and made the decision that I was moving to Tuscany. I was so excited by my decision that I turned on the computer and along with my Christmas message to everyone I also included my decision to move to Tuscany. I don't know if I was looking for validation on my decision or waiting for one of my kids to have me committed. Either way, I had already hit the send button and the message was out.

Needless to say the phone started ringing off the wall once the e-mail was read. My son-in-law, Robbie and my daughter, Christy, sent me an e-mail of the following they found on the internet:

A Life with a View
By Paula Harris
I woke up this morning
And I decided I am moving
To Tuscany

I'm moving to Tuscany
To own a vineyard
That stretches out as far
As the sunset
And to live in a villa
That sees all of this

I am moving to Tuscany
To make beautiful wines
Although, I don't drink
Myself
That will be acclaimed
Worldwide

I am moving to Tuscany
Where I'll master the language
In a day
At most,
After all
I do have some Italian blood

I am moving to Tuscany
Where each day
I'll walk to the farmer's market
Holding a cane basket in the crook
Of my arm
Buying produce to supplement
My own garden of vegtables
Fruits and herb

I am moving to Tuscany
To host dinner parties
That people will scramble
To be invited to,
Indulging in delectable conversation
and food to match

I am moving to Tuscany
To meet beautiful Mediterranean men
And to take them all
As lovers
One at a time
Or in groups

I am moving to Tuscany
To eat crostini
For brunch each day
With prosciutto sliced too thick
And I'll even learn to like
Cannellini beans
Once I'm in Tuscany

With my decision now made to move to Tuscany came the idea of living in Cortona. This decision led to a million things I would have to do to make the move possible. I had collected 50 years of furniture and other stuff, two dogs, a house and a car that either needed to be sold, stored or taken with me. It dawned on me the more you own, the more you are owned! All of the things we amass in our lives keep us from going anywhere, on a long term basis, or doing anything that might jeopardize the things we own. It was time to clean house!

My first thought was I needed a place to live in Cortona. I sent off e-mails to two agents I had met during my visit in September. Hoping I would hear from them soon, I was able to move on to other things. Do I sell my house, furniture and car? Do I put things in storage? Do I give all of my furniture and other belongings to the kids? All of these things had to be addressed and taken care of in some manner.

Weeks went by; I finally heard from both of the agents and they told me apartments would become available in April or May. Would that work for me? What size did I need? How much did I want to pay? How soon was I planning on moving to Cortona? I really didn't know any of the answers. I just knew I wanted to go to Cortona. I vaguely answered all of their questions and thought I'd just let the chips fall (as mom would say).

Well, the chips did fall. I got a contract on my house which included all of my furniture, paintings, books, down to my pots and pans. I also had someone who wanted to buy my car. Lucy would come with me and Jake would stay with my daughter, Carrie.

This wild idea of mine was moving way too fast. I told Lenny, the man who had contracted to buy my house, that I needed to think about the offer and I would get back to him in a few days. I did not commit to selling the car. After walking around my house, many, many times and thinking things through and reviewing my budget, I decided not to sell anything. I thought it made much more sense to close the house up and let the kid's look in on it, keep my furniture and car. It was settled. I would go to Cortona for one year and not sell anything.

If I decided I wanted to make Cortona my permanent home, after a year, I would return and sell everything at that time. All I had to do was have a place to live and I would be ready to leave. I just received an e-mail from Roberto; a perfect apartment is coming available, can I come now? Yes, I can come now!

# CRAZY SALLY

When I was living that nutty life as a real estate broker, making a ton of money, I had a re-curring dream for years. In that dream I was a bag lady living on the streets of New York City. I dubbed this crazy lady, my muse, as Crazy Sally. Crazy Sally, my muse, my inspiration, my imagination is still with me, only I am no longer a 'bag lady.' Now Crazy Sally comes to me when I am quiet, still, in a rut or just doing nothing with my life.

Crazy Sally visits me when I am down on life, unhappy or undecided as to what to do with my life. I never found the peace, as most people do, in traditional life, marriage, family or in a career. Every time my life gets to that point, along comes Crazy Sally to shake me up and change my life.

One might think I can shut Crazy Sally up or ignore her. Impossible! She just gets louder and louder. She won't go away and she makes me go out and live life. I've come to love and appreciate my muse. If not for her, I would just be someone's wife, mother or employee.

Thanks to Crazy Sally, I get to really live life for everything I can squeeze out of it. So, in fact, my life is like a lemon, but I have enough juice for the squeeze.

Crazy Sally showed up on the eve after mother's death while I was sitting in a chair, thinking about mom, life, divorce and death. I kept telling her to go away, that I wanted to sink in my misery and feel sorry for myself, my life and mom's death. That's when Crazy Sally went crazy, and became as loud as ever. She spent days with me and she was relentless until I made the decision to change my life and to move to Cortona, Italy.

# Via Maffei 11

*Via Maffei 11*, 52044 Cortona, AR Italia is my new address, *per il periodo dal 1 Giugno 2005 al 31 Maggio 2006.*

On the eve of my move to Cortona, I was packed, had been for a week, and excited about spending a year in Italy. I know little of the town, having only visited once, and nothing of my apartment except that it is located 'center city.' Center City sounds great to me, as I am not much of a walker. I'm more into Yoga and Pilates, great exercise on level ground.

I arrived at DFW International Airport three hours before my departure. I wanted to make sure I had enough time to check in and have a proper "smokethon" prior to having nine and a half hours of a smoke free environment.

Quay took me to the airport and stayed for awhile, then Carrie (my daughter) stayed with me until it was time to board the plane. Quay and I had a great chuckle while checking in my luggage.

The baggage inspector, with his very southern drawl (I should have understood him, as I am also from the south) asked if I had any farms in my luggage?

I looked at him and wondered what drugs he was taking but replied," Well possibly, if dirt on my shoes from my garden constitutes a 'farm.'"

"Ma'am, that'd be fire arms."

We both laughed and I thought, oh my, if I don't understand the language here whatever will I do in Italy!

Prior to boarding the plane I had a small moment of panic, wondering if I really knew what I was doing and if I could handle the luggage, learn to speak the language, and learn how to survive in a world I was so unaccustomed to. I took a deep breathe and told myself to be brave, all was good.

With the heightened security at the airports, they now confiscate your lighters. A man who had just gotten off the plane approached me and asked for a light. I noticed he had a very nice Italian accent and told him I was moving to Cortona. He took his passport out of his breast pocket, turned to the information page and showed me where it said he was born in Cortona. Small world; his name is Oriano Petrucci and now lives in Coppell, Texas. He gave me names of people to contact and places to eat. I gave him my address in Cortona and told him to drop in anytime.

The seat on the plane next to me was occupied by a German man, living in Switzerland, with terrible bad breath, stuff in his teeth, who talked non-stop and passed gas the entire way to Paris. I am not talking about those tiny silent farts with a small odor that we have all experienced. I am talking about loud, disgusting passing of gas, with a smell so bad that I had to cover my nose and hope I would not projectile vomit onto the hair of the person in front of me. This man was winning prizes for his farts and I couldn't just sit by without comment.

I finally said to him, "Are you passing gas and would you not be more comfortable in the bathroom?"

He said, "It's a natural body function and I just have a little gas from the American food."

"Man, that is not a little gas. That is intoxication by lethal fumes."

The plane was full or I would have moved. Any thoughts of my taking a nap, as it was a night flight, were completely taken away by this man. I couldn't wait to get to Paris.

Once at Paris de Gaulle airport, this man would not leave my side. He insisted on walking me five terminals, where I was to board my plane to *Firenze*. Upon arriving at my gate, he suggested coffee. I tried to decline the offer but he just insisted. I knew his connecting flight left from terminal B, we were at F, in one hour, so I excused myself to the bathroom where I stayed for 45 minutes.

The flight from Paris to *Firenze* (Florence) takes two hours and the flight was listed as "meal details not available" operated by Air France. In the States, we are used to peanuts and a coke on short flights, so it was no surprise to find 'meal details not available' and I fully expected the flight service to be like in the States.

I had never flown Air France and was a bit concerned when they bused us out on the tarmac to board the plane . We passed very small planes and I started to count the number of people on the bus to determine just how small our plane might be. I was nervous about boarding a tiny plane.

To my delight the plane was a British Aerospace Jet, seating about a hundred people. To my further delight the seats were big and roomy and they served real food. Imagine this, I was served an espresso, peanut sauce dipped chicken on a stick, a roll, a quiche, and a warm cherry tart. I want to always fly Air France.

I arrived in *Firenze* at two in the afternoon and by this time I had been on the move for eighteen hours and was very tired.

*Firenze* International Airport is very small. No customs that I saw. I just picked up my luggage and walked out of the airport.

When I exited the airport, the taxi stand was right there so I inquired, *"Quanto costa la tassi va Cortona?"*

He replied, *"About duecento euros."* That's about $240 plus tip for a one hour car trip.

I thought about it for a moment. I was tired and the money seemed worth the trip but I would not get the local travel experience and that is what this entire new lifestyle is about. I declined and jumped on the autobus to Santa Maria Novella Treno Stazione.

I took the treno regionale to Camucia, taking an hour and a half. From the *stazione* in Camucia I took another autobus up the hill to Cortona.

I departed the autobus from a parking lot outside of Cortona. Thankfully the autobus stop was at the entrance of Via Nazionale, the street my estate agent has his office. Via Nazionale is a flat street *"Ruga Piana"* and with all of my luggage, I was forever grateful. I was lugging two large suitcases, a laptop briefcase, a backpack and a large purse. All of my luggage is Louis Vuitton and suddenly I felt like a walking, live commercial for Louis Vuitton. That was not the image I wanted.

I found my estate agent's office without trouble, just inside the walls of Cortona. Roberto (my agent) was at his desk when I walked in with all my luggage. I proceeded to drop the luggage and tell him that the trip (now 21 hours) wasn't so bad.

As in most European cities, the stores close from 1–4 every afternoon for siesta. Roberto had been in his office only a little over an hour awaiting my arrival. I signed all of the necessary papers and we were off to see my new apartment.

My apartment at Via Maffei 11, was built in 1505 and had been remodeled two years ago. I told all of my friends that Maffei was pronounced 'mafia.' I stand corrected, it is really pronounced "mafay."

Roberto took my two large suitcases, leaving me with my backpack, laptop bag and big purse, saying *"Andiamo!"*

So off we went. We walked about two blocks on this lovely, flat, narrow street with shops and cafés along either side into a large Piazza (the Piazza della Republica). I was loving this, and I was on a great energy high.

Once we were in the Piazza I realized many of the streets off the Piazza were going up hill. I don't mean a slight graceful incline, I mean San Francisco style uphill! I was hoping one of those streets would not be mine. My hopes dashed, Roberto headed up the steepest of them all. I could only follow in his foot steps and hope it would not be far. I managed that first hill and Roberto took a right onto another yet steeper hill (Via Maffei) and my only question was, "How far up this street is my apartment?"

We made it; we were finally standing at the front door of my apartment building. My thoughts of giving away everything I owned on the trip up those hills were now in the back of my head. I could just relax and enjoy being here. Thank goodness for my Yoga and Pilates and being thin. I could only imagine that I would never leave my apartment to face the long uphill battle to return back home.

Roberto was smiling and I, I was huffing and puffing. I told Roberto, "I am glad that is over!"

He laughed, opened the door and said, "Not yet. Your apartment is on *Piano tre*!"

"What? The third floor you say, that's impossible!"

Roberto unlocked the door, sat my luggage down said, *"Arrivederci,"* and was gone.

Left alone to inspect my apartment, I was as full of excitement as if I had just entered my first dorm room at university. My apartment is a small two bedroom with one bath; I think about 60m in Italian terms. When you enter the front door, you are in one room serving as the kitchen, dining and living areas. From there you enter a wide hall which leads to the two bedrooms and bath. There is no central heat and air, no microwave, no dishwasher, no trash compactor and no clothes dryer, nor do I have a bathtub. However, I do have a bidet and several art niches. The ceilings in my apartment are brick with two-by-four's running lengthwise and twelve-by-twelve center beams every eight feet. The floors are brick tiles in a crisscross pattern, which I am sure are cold as ice in the winter. The walls are stucco that have been whitewashed. The apartment has a beautiful heavy wood, double door with exposed hinges and big door knockers and the interior doors are of the same heavy wood with antique handles and keys.

The windows are large with heavy wood exterior, slatted shutters and glass panes with interior solid wood shutters. I am assuming all of this will keep the winds and drafts out during the winter. The exterior walls are two feet thick and the interior walls are half as thick. All of the windows (screenless), are wide open, and nice fresh air is felt throughout the apartment, which I am sure the flies adore. The furniture is early college. I jumped on the bed to see if it is nice and soft; to my disappointment, I think it is made of straw. There are of course no closets; only armoires in which to hang my clothes. All and all, I like it and think I will do just fine living here.

I was really tired but wanted a shower, to get something to eat and go to bed. I headed for the bathroom to take a quick shower. No such thing as a quick shower in Italy . First of all, the shower is very small and must be made of some plastic material as the bottom gets very slick. I got a routine going, of sorts; the shower head is hand held, so I wet myself, hang up the head, soap down, rinse off. I must do these steps about three times to get the job done. Even at this I have not washed my feet or shaved my legs. Okay, next step is to get out of the shower, fill a pail with warm water, soak my feet while shaving, put my feet back in the shower to rinse and walla! I am *finito*! Guys, a little advice before you visit, do not push your wives to get ready in a hurry, it just can't happen.

I have a TV, but no telephone. I leave my TV on all the time and watch things like "Two and a Half Men" in Italian. The show is funny in English but funnier in Italian (I think).

The first thing I wanted to get for my apartment was a telephone. I thought, like in the U.S., you just go out and do it. So I got up early on the second day and headed out to get a telephone.

My first lesson was learning store hours. The stores do not open until 9:00 am (it was only 8:00); they stay open until one and close from one to four, re-opening at four and remain open until seven or eight.

My choices were to walk back up the hill to my apartment or sit at a sidewalk café until the stores open. The café won out, hands down!

While having coffee, I asked the waiter where I needed to go for a telephone. He asked me if the wiring had been installed? I told him I didn't have any idea but it should by as my *appartamento* is after all over 500 years old. He then asked me for my address (I wondered if he was going to install my phone).

I gave him my address and he said, "Oh, no that building has never been wired, you must seek an electrician."

Obviously my next question was *"Dove?"* (where)

He said, "I have cousin for you, let me make a call."

Five minutes later, Luigi appeared from nowhere and informed me he was an electrician and he would maybe help me.

Oh my, that's easy. No, it's not! First he tells me, the job is too small for his time so I tell him, "Ah, but my doorbell and my downstairs intercom are in need of repair too."

Then he says, "Okay signora. I can do it Monday," and departed.

I was left wondering if he meant next Monday or some Monday in the distant future. In hopes that Luigi did mean next Monday, I went home and snipped the wires on my doorbell and my intercom so the job would be big enough.

While I was disengaging my doorbell and intercom I was thinking about all of the articles I had read on how difficult it was to get things done in Italy and feeling pleased that I had mastered getting things done when no one else had seemed to be able to.

Well, Monday came and went and so did Luigi.

When Luigi got to my apartment he asked me for my *contratto* and my *residente* card. I had neither! Luigi explained to me these were needed before he could perform any work on providing wiring for a telephone. He did not know how to obtain these items, just that they were required by the *ufficiale.'*

I told him, "Okay, but could you fix my doorbell and intercom while you are here?"

He said, "*Non*, job too *piccolo!*"

Well darn, don't come ringing my doorbell!

# Mal di Denti

I am in pain and have been all night. I haven't slept and have been taking pain medication through out the night. I brought an extra strength pain reliever with me. It is 500 mg to reduce pain and fever. One tablet was keeping the pain from my toothache tolerable but now I am taking three and it's not really helping. My upper lip is swollen as well, as are my eyes. The pain or infection is affecting my sinus cavities and it hurts to move my lip. I was in bad shape and needed to go to the farmacia. I decided before making the walk into town to make my lista of new words and phrases for the day.

Mi lista read like this:

| | |
|---|---|
| *Mal di denti.* | I have a toothache. |
| *Io avere ascess o infezione denti.* | I have an abscess or infection in my tooth. |
| *Lei aiuto mi, per favore?* | Can you help me, please? |

*Mi parola:*

| | |
|---|---|
| *Infezione* | *infection* |
| *Io dolere* | *I hurt* |
| *Antibiotico* | *antibiotics* |
| *Dentista* | |
| *Appuntamento* | *appointment* |

When I arrived at the pharmacy I used all of the words on my list trying to make sure they understood my needs. They told me at the pharmacy they could not give me antibiotics without a prescription but they could give me an anti-inflammatory. I said I would take it, gave him 4.5 *euros* and he told me to eat before I took them.

I asked if there was a dentista ecco en Cortona.

"*Si, ecco en Cortona* up the street from the post office."

I stopped at Café di Artista for coffee and a croissant. I wanted to get food in me as fast as possible so I could take one of the pills. Gino, a man I had met on my first day in Cortona, came by my table to chat and I shared with him my *mal di denti*. He offered to walk me to the dentist office.

He said, "Take my arm, *esso es molto romantico!*"

Romance was far from my mind.

By this time I had taken the pills and was wondering what effect an unknown drug would have on me and I wished I could have read the label warnings, two pages of warnings. I had real trepidations about making an *appuntamento* at the *dentista*.

I had just had experience with businesses operating without a license. The I-net bar I go to, to send and receive my e-mails, had not been opened for four days. I would go three or four times a day just to make sure I was going during hours he was opened. Yesterday there was a business card from the Inspector *Ufficiale*.

I asked Giovanni, the local tour guide, "What does that mean?"

He said, "He is probably operating the business without a license."

That's very common here in Cortona! Italy's education system is very different from ours. Going through high school is the same as four years of college in the States. Meaning when you complete high school, you are certified to teach, to enter medical school or to enter dental school. Some professionals practice medicine or dentistry without a license. Now I felt really great about going to the dentist.

Arm and arm Gino and I walked to the dentist office. Me feeling drugged and scared, and Gino feeling *romantico!* At the post office, we took a right up a street so steep they have even installed a rail to hold on to and steps.

Gino says, "The *dentista* is at the top."

Gee, everything is at the top. Halfway up this hill I was grateful for Gino's arm and told him so. We got to the top and found the dentist's office but it is closed. There was no sign with posted hours or days of operation. I looked closely to make sure the Inspector *Ufficiale* had not left a card. Gino suggested he take me to Camucia or Arezzo to the *dentista* but I declined. I was thinking he just wants more *romantico* and I just wanted to lie down.

I told him *arrivederci*, and headed back to Via Maffei 11.

By this time the pills I had taken have helped. The swelling has gone down and I can now move my lip. I think to myself, maybe I can go a little longer before I have to see the *dentista*!

# Castiglion del Lago
## Lago Trasimeno

Castiglion del Lago was not to be the first city I wanted to visit in the Tuscany area. Actually, it is not even located in Tuscany, it is in Umbria bordering Tuscany. I had planned at some point to visit because of the well known lake, Lago Trasimeno, but it did not rank number one on my list.

I was forced by *"mal de denti"* (a toothache) to seek this beautiful town out. I was almost at panic stage when someone in Cortona told me of a *dentista* in Castiglion del Lago that was English.

It was 7:30 in the evening when I was given the name of the dentist.

I purchased a phone card, and called immediately. I did not expect to get an answer at his office but thought I could find out the office hours. In fact, the message referred me to his cell phone.

He answered on the first ring, to my great pleasure. I told him I had just moved to Cortona.

He said, "Well welcome."

I said, "Oh, but the reason I am calling is because of *mal di denti.*" I told him it was infected or something and I was in serious pain.

He called the *farmacia* in Cortona for pain pills and told me to be at his office at 9:30 domani (tomorrow), on his day off.

The bus from Cortona takes you to Camucia, on to Terontola. From Terontola, I took a train to Castiglion del Lago and I made a 15 minute walk up (everything is up) to town center and there was his office.

When I walked into the waiting area, a dental assistant came out, took my information and told me to have a seat and Roger would be right with me. My dentist office at home is a high-tech office with eight assistants, computers reading the x-rays, nice gas, never knowing you have had a shot. They always schedule my appointments at ten so, on the overhead TV, I can watch Price is Right.

Easy! Was I wrong to expect not much less?

After about five minutes, the door opened and standing there was a man in white jodhpurs, flat red tennis shoes, no socks, an apron and latex gloves. I thought he had come to clean the toilets.

But no, he introduced himself as the dentist. "Pleased to meet you."

Now aside from his outfit, he is a beautiful man. Blonde, blue-eyed, medium height, nice body and great legs. But, is this really proper dress for a *dentista*?

I guess so, you see, things are a little more casual in Italy. We chatted for a few minutes then he took an x-ray of my tooth. While we waited the ten minutes for the x-rays, he made us espresso and we stepped out onto a small terrace overlooking the lake. I enjoyed a cigarette and the conversation, him saying bloke and me saying ya'll.

He only has one room, other than the small reception area, which functions as the examination room, his office and I guess the espresso room. His office looks out on the lake, and if things were not high-tech, it was spotlessly clean. Comforting!

The x-rays revealed a small abscess. He drilled a tiny hole in the top back of my tooth for drainage, prescribed antibiotics and said, "Wait a few days, let it drain and then we will decide if we need to do a root canal."

I opened my purse, preparing to pay him when he said, "Let's just wait and see what has to be done. If we must do a root canal it will cost about 90 euros but don't pay me today." That would never happen in America! I was thrilled that I was not going to lose the tooth and that I was pain free.

He then asked me if I had time for him to show me around town and we could have a nice lunch before my train back to Camucia? Wow, I think I am going to love my *dentista* in Italia.

The Information Office in Castiglion del Lago provided me with the following information:

Castiglion del Lago, since Etruscan times, the area under the dominion of Chiusi, has concentrated mainly on agriculture, especially the production of grain. Around the seventh century, Castiglione's promontory and peninsula provided the Tuscian Lombards with a for-midable defensive position against Byzantine Perugia.

The town was fought over by Arezzo, Cortona and Perugia, Perugia finally running out the victor. In 1247, Frederick II of Swabia conquered the town and rebuilt it as it is today. This Franciscan friar was also the architect of the Rocca del Leone (Lion Fortress), in the form of a pentagon with four corner towers and a keep on a triangular plan. The building, one of the finest examples of medieval military architecture in Umbria, is situated on a spur of limestone rock which gives it complete dominion over Lake Trasimeno. A delightful covered walkway connects the fortress to the Renaissance Della Corgna Palace. The Palace was built for Ascanio dell Corgna, who in 1563 received the title of Marquis of Castiglion del Lago and Chiugi from his uncle, Pope Julius III del Monte. The interior of the Palace, designed by the Perugian architect Galeazzo Alessi, is extensively decorated with frescoes, many of them by the Tuscan painter Niccolo Circignani, known as 'Il Pomarancio'. Isola Polvese,' the largest island in the lake, also belongs to Castiglion del Lago. Particularly noteworthy are the fifteenth century Abbey of San Secondo, the Castle and the Church of St. Julia.

Castiglion del Lago is known for Coloiamo I Cieli, (Let's colour the skies), where kites of all types are flown on the lakeside.

Being large but shallow, Lake Trasimeno, at 128 square kilometers, the fourth largest Italian lake in area, is a haven for a wide variety of birds. The lake is surrounded by a flat, alluvial plain, then a ring of gentle hills, where woodland alternates with fields of sunflowers and maize, vineyards and olive groves. In the thirteenth century, some masters of glass-working from Venice, attracted by the plentiful supply of timber and water, needed for the art of glass-making, transformed Piegaro into a notable glass-working center. By the fifteenth century, several towns had achieved a certain amount of fame and a high level of economic and cultural life, giving rise to the artistic genius of Masolino of Panicale and Pietro Vannucci of Citta' della Pieve, known as Il Perugino In 1995 the Umbria Region established the Lake Trasimeno Natural Park, with its headquarter at Passignano sul Trasimeno. It said, "Lake Trasimeno, a place where earth, air and water are unaffected by pollution, and men, birds and fish can follow lives in peace."

# Wash Day in Cortona

Once I made the decision to move to Cortona, I read and searched the internet for all the information I could find on the town, the people and any other interesting facts. In doing so, I ran across a great picture of an aging Cortonese woman, cigarette dangling from her mouth, leaning out a window (appearing to be two to three stories up) of her apartment, hanging the wash on a suspended clothesline. I laughed, thinking this picture was taken 50 or so years ago. Gee I am glad we have advanced so far and now have dryers. *That aging woman is me today!*

I wrote friends and family, I told people here in Cortona and I put it in my journal right after seeing my apartment for the first time that I did not have a dryer. I just did not think about what it meant not to have a dryer.

Well on my first wash day in Cortona, I placed my clothes in the washing machine, filled it with soap, read an instruction booklet (in Italian) and finally learned how to get it going. It washed, and washed and washed. I did not want to turn it off as I could see through the front glass door that soapy water was still in the machine. I decided not to watch the pot boil, to just let it do its thing and I would go to the piazza for coffee and visit with the people. If it is still running after a day or two, I would call someone. I was like a man not wanting to stop and ask for directions.

In town, I ran across Jamie. Now Jamie is a strange guy. He says he's from California in one conversation and from Santa Fe in another. In one conversation he told me he had, for a short time, owned a restaurant in Sante Fe. When asked what type of cuisine, he said he didn't worry about the food he would occasionally sell a cup of coffee and a cigarette. Jamie is strange.

Jamie is married to Lisabette (he also says that's her real name but it may be like me saying I live on a street pronounced Mafia). Maybe, Lisabette is Elizabeth in Italian. I have never seen or met Lisabette but he talks about her as though she is real, so maybe there is a Lisabette. Anyway, Jamie is a writer and his wife is an artist and photographer. I asked Jamie if Lisabette has showings at any of the local galleries (there are about twenty galleries in Cortona) and he tells me that no, she only paints by commission. It leads me to wonder how you can photograph if you don't go out of the house, and how you can commission art if you don't show and when Jamie might write, since he is always in the Piazza. But like I said, Jamie is strange.

Only months later would I find how sage the advice was from Jamie; that Lisabette is not Elizabeth in Italian. It is Lisabette and what a great photographer she is and I learned of her wonderful reputation as an artist.

Jamie and Lisabette have the greatest apartment location in Cortona. Above the post office are three stories of apartments. Their apartment is on the top, with large windows overlooking the main Piazza. They do not have a garden terrace but the apartment beneath them does. Looking out of their big windows they have a great view of the garden terrace and the piazza. The garden terrace is as big as my entire apartment and filled with the most glorious flowers. Great view and they get it for free and without the maintenance. Next time I move to Cortona, I want their apartment. Lucky!

Well, I had been gone for more than two hours so surely my wash had finished. I trudged back up to my apartment, opened the door and didn't hear the machine running. Wash complete.

My landlady has thought of everything for my apartment including a laundry basket. I took the clothes out of the washing machine, shake them and put them in the basket. It then hit me, *I DO NOT HAVE A DRYER!* I seriously, do not have a dryer!

I left my apartment, made a complete search of all three floors looking for a door or cubby hole where a dryer might be. There is no dryer!

I don't remember seeing any laundromat anywhere in town. What do people do with their wet clothes? I causally look up, suspended clotheslines! I went back up to *Piano tre* and entered my apartment. I know there is not a suspended clothesline outside of the living room window because I spend a great deal of time (and pleasure) at that window watching people huff and puff their way up my street. I check my bedroom window, not there, so it must be outside my second bedroom window, a window I have never opened.

I opened the inside shutter, the window, force back the outside shutter and there it is my very own suspended clothesline. It is a two line system with some type of pulley apparatus and I am not just real sure how it works but I have to find out because I need more than the three feet of line that is just outside the window. I am leaning out of the window trying to get a handle on things when I notice that MY suspended clothesline reaches across my neighbor's window.

What does this mean, do we share the clothesline or is it a way for him (my neighbor) to steal my panties. And speaking of my panties, if I hang them on the line, everyone walking past the piazza is going to be able to view my panties.

Now, I have never used a clothesline before but I do remember, when I was very young, my *nonna* telling me clothes smelled so fresh from the clothesline. So okay, they will smell really fresh but unless you are going to walk around with your nose in your clothes, what great thing is this wonderful smell about. Well my clothes are now washed and hanging on my clothesline and I am waiting for that wonderful fresh smell when it starts to rain. Now what do I do? Leave them on the line or bring them in the house, or what? Well wait a minute, my *nonna* also used to tell me that rain water was really good for your hair and would make it soft. Hey, if it works for hair it must work for clothes! My clothes stayed on the line for two days until the rain finally stopped. I was anticipating soft clothes that would smell great!

I ran into Giovanni, Amy's husband and local tour guide, after my clothes had been on the line for more than a day. He told me during his tours that every time he passes my apartment he tells the tour group that the lady with the clothes hanging on the line in the rain is a crazy lady from America.

I say, "Thanks Giovanni, and I will get you back."

The part of the joke that Giovanni does not tell me about, I hear at breakfast. There were two English couples at the table next to mine taking about this wonderful tour guide, the best they have ever had, during the tour while passing an apartment he says, "Look up, see the undergarments hanging on the clothesline, she's a crazy lady from America and does not know that we do not hang our undergarments outside for all to see. We hang them on a drying rack in our bathrooms!" (I guess my landlady forgot to supply me one thing, the drying rack) I wanted to lean over and say, "I am that crazy lady from America."

Well, tomorrow will be Giovanni's day. I bought a pair of very large (300 lb. guy size) boxer shorts and a black magic marker. I wrote Giovanni's on the back of this large pair of underwear and tomorrow they and they alone will be hanging on my clothesline. Ha, ha, Giovanni!

# Prima Settimana a Cortona
## Scarpe e Denti
*First Week in Cortona*
*Shoes and Teeth*

One could never imagine one's life could change so much in a mere week. I have a much greater appreciation of religion, art, shoes and teeth. In my former life, I woke between five and five-thirty and was in bed by ten. Never a night owl and always a morning person, I would never imagine a change.

Here, in Cortona, in only a few days it all changed. I don't eat dinner until 8:00 and it's a two hour affair putting me in bed never before midnight and at times much later. Going to bed past midnight makes mornings late, usually after nine. Nine is a perfect time to get out of bed and start your day.

The stores, other than cafes and the market, don't open until nine. I am certain when I have spoken of the streets of Cortona, one would imagine streets like at home only, in the case of Dallasites, uphill. Not true; the streets of Cortona are really more like alleyways, the locals call them alleys. The alleys are made of stone and very uneven. The alleys date as far back as the 1200's. Not only do they go straight up or straight down they are also very narrow and when cars come you learn quickly to hug the buildings. My first journey up the alleys, I wondered why they were so uneven, leaving one very unsure footed. Well now it makes perfect sense, how could you walk up and down if they were smooth, one would never get up and always be sliding down. The conditions of the alleys make you cautious of the shoes you wear. I brought eight pairs with me, rejected four pairs the first 15 minutes, reducing me to four pairs. I have tried all four pairs, three pairs of sandals and one pair of loafers.

The two pairs of sandals with stacked heels are forever making my ankles turn (causing great pain) and a fear of breakage. One pair of flat sandals made the bones of my feet feel as though they are coming through the bottoms of my feet.

That leaves me the loafers. The loafers are comfortable and seem to keep me upright on the alleys but they just don't go with everything. Alas, I have found a *Calzature* (shoestore) at the bottom of my street. Franco is the store owner and an agreeable guy. He says *si, si* to my every word. He doesn't carry many shoes in size five and a half, but *si, si*, he will order more. He loves to put shoes on my feet, and take them off. He says, "*Si, si*, very nice feet." When I walk around his store in shoes he has put on my feet, he says, "*Si, si*, very comfortable," and "*Si, si bello* on your feet." He's very agreeable. I still haven't found the perfect shoe but my search will continue. I mean, what could be better than Italian made shoes!

Now teeth; when we are in our fifties, teeth become very important. As young adults and thirty year olds we love the eyes. The eyes tell so many things, can be very sexy, and most informative. Yes, love those eyes. But now, at my age, it is most definitely the teeth. I always thought it was the French with bad teeth. Not so; it is a condition of Europe in general.

My third day in Cortona I was stricken with *mal di denti*, a toothache, and became very aware of the teeth of the Cortonese. I became certain that the only thing the *dentista* here do to people's teeth is clean them or pull them and I wasn't real sure about the cleaning part. I started having dreams that I was forced to go to the *dentista* here and not understanding one another, he put me to sleep, pulled by tooth, and when I woke up, he said, "Yes now you look like the locals." To make my fear of the *dentista* even more cemented, I was having coffee yesterday at Café di Artista and there was a very attractive gentleman two tables over who kept looking at me and smiling. He eventually approached to chat me up. When he opened his mouth to speak to me, egads! He had teeth missing. I think two, but I could not look at him to make sure.

I just said, "*Non parlo l'italiano*," and looked down at my menu. He walked off saying (I think), "*Non parlo italiano but leggere l'italiano*."

God, give me a pretty man with good teeth.

That is not to say all of the Cortonese have bad teeth. In fact, the

Cortonese are some of the most beautiful people in the world. The young girls and women would make most of you older guys grab your heart pills or the little blue ones. The men, some with long black wavy hair and others with straight blonde hair, are sexy and heartthrobs. I have met and chatted over dinner with some of the most elegant and beautiful people. I think the beauty of the people of Cortona is a reflection of the beauty of the art in Cortona.

Some of the most impressive art by the most influential artists is located in the Churches and Museums of Cortona. In my daily walks, I have visited twelve of the twenty-eight churches, the Duomo and Le Celle.

Not believing myself to be particularly religious by nature, I was stunned at the feelings the Duomo, the Churches and the Le Celle stirred in me. I can't help to becoming tearful and to sit and pray for long periods at a time.

I spent most of my first week in Cortona, only venturing out of town on my second day. I took a bus to the COOP in Camucia to get the essentials for my apartment, like water, tea, coffee, a watch (I left the Rolex at home, thinking it pretentious in Cortona) and an alarm clock.

While shopping, I did not consider how I was going to get the things I bought back up the hills to my apartment.

Oh my goodness, how difficult can one's life become? It was treacherous and I quickly decided I must find a market that would deliver. I did; I found just that perfect market in Piazza della Repubblica, Market Molesini, owned by Marco Molesini and family. In my broken Italian I asked them if they delivered. They said, "*Si*, just give us *a lista oggi* (today) and we will deliver *domani* (tomorrow) around *all' una* (1:00)." A *lista* was all I needed. Okay, so I will prepare a *lista* in English and translate it to Italiano. *No problemo.*

*Ecco es mi lista*!

*Due grandi bottiglie d'acqua naturale*

*Un pane*

*Un piccolo latte*

*Zucchero*
*Sapone (una saponetta)*
*Marmellata*
*Burro*
*Un portacenere*
*Della carta igienica*
*Un succo di frutta all'arancia*
*Due bottiglie di vino rosso*
*Due bottiglie di vino bianco*
*Finito!*

My items were delivered the next day at one, he asked me for 50 euros (I think, wow that's a lot). I gave him the 50 euros and he gave me a sack that had been tied with my receipt and change for 50 euros. Easy!

Getting my hair done was just about as easy as buying my groceries. I went to David and Francesco and explained to them, in broken *Italiano*, that I wanted a wash, conditioner and blow dry but no haircut and no color. I think my *Italiano* translated to, "Please cut my conditioner and add no color to it," but they seem to understand and told me to come back at *sono le cinque e venti*. I returned at 5:20 and they took me to the shampoo bowl and I got the finest head massage. She then wrapped my hair in a towel and instructed me to go to the stylist chair. At the stylist chair, Francesco came over with a bowl of purple foam and started putting it on my hair.

I said, *"Basta! Basta!"* Thinking I was saying stop in Italian when really, I was saying enough!

"I do not want color on my hair."

He laughed and said, "No, no color, it is your conditioner."

All went well and my hair never looked better.

Before my move to Cortona, in order to learn Italian, I listened to tapes, read books and did assignments in workbooks and was never without my flash cards. Once in Cortona my system changed. I use five new words and three new phrases no less than ten times a day. I write the words and phrases and the meanings on a piece of paper and carry it with me wherever I go. Until noon I am always looking at that piece of paper trying to remember the words and how exactly to use them. One of my favorite words of my list is *Basta!* Which means to stop, actually it means that's enough but I always use it when I want something to stop. I always say it twice, *Basta! Basta*! And when using this word you must curl four fingers and touch your thumb with the curled fingers making an O and wave you hand at the same time, unless of course, you are using this to stop an approaching car, then you would put your hand out flat and say, loudly, *"Basta! Basta!"* Very Italian, don't you think?

Now, my system is that I have to use this word, any word, ten times in one day. But because I always say *"Basta, Basta"* that is only considered using the word once. It's so delicious; I really get to say *Basta, Basta* twenty times in one day.

There are some things everyone should be aware of before visiting Italy. It is not acceptable to drink cappuccino after the morning hours. You must drink espresso or if you just must have milk in your coffee it is not all right, but acceptable to order caffé *macchiato.* When saying grazie, never pronounce it with a "t" in it. Many, who do not speak *italiano,* say *gratze,* wrong and never say (very often pronounced this way) graze. And never ask for a doggie bag if you do not finish your meal. This is an insult to the chef. I don't know why, nor do I know what they do with all the leftover food (What's in my soup?) (proportions are *molto grande*) but I do know, not to do it!

I wake up every morning with the aroma of flowers: poppies, azaleas, and roses; herbs: rosemary, basil, and thyme; and fresh breads baking. I can now tell my children where capers come from, wonderful, small bushes growing out of the walls of Cortona.

The Cortonese are like the flowers of Cortona; some grow wild like the poppies while yet others are lovingly planted and gingerly taken care of, like the roses. I have had the pleasure, in my short time here, to meet both. They are wonderful, delightful people with hearts of gold. I tell them I live here, on a street pronounced Mafia. They all laugh and tell me, "Non, your street is pronounced Mafay and you don't live here, yet. You are not a local, not yet a resident but you are not a tourist, either." They tell me after I get through my first November, then I will be a resident and live in Cortona. I still go around saying that I live in Cortona, on a street pronounced Mafia.

There are many tourist visiting this time of year and many people from all countries who live here part of the year. University of Georgia has the art school here with visiting professors. I met one of the profs and have enjoyed visiting with him. He came here as a visiting professor from UGA ten years ago, and fell in love. He is an art prof and film director for the school. He loved Cortona so much that he has lived here every summer for the past ten years. He has long hair worn in a ponytail, films nude art and tells all of the young girls of his hippie, orgy days. I tell him he tells of these stories to the young girls for either shock value or the hope of sleeping with them or both. He asked me if it worked for me, if I would sleep with him, and I tell him, "No, my hippie days are long gone and I'm looking for someone younger."

So we both have found a friendship where we talk of our younger years and our feelings of Europe today.

Londoners didn't visit here much until the movie and the book *Under the Tuscan Sun*; now they come in droves. They all come wanting to throw pennies in the fountain, not knowing the fountain was a special effect. I am amazed that this small hilltop town, Cortona, is found and loved by so many. This time of year the population triples with visitors moving in and out on a daily basis until the end of September or middle of October, weather permitting.

When I visited Cortona last September, I met a great couple from New Jersey. They had found their way to Cortona three years ago, rented the same house every season and when the house came on the market, they bought it and are now owners of their own home and vineyard. I ran into them on Monday. They had just arrived for the season and will be staying until the end of September. They were surprised that I had found my way back and had rented an apartment for a year.

I met another couple from L.A. who have been residing here off and on for five years. Each year they extend their stay longer and longer. She is an artist and he a writer. Katerina, an artist friend of mine that I met last September, just told me about a couple in Montepulciano, a town near here, who are from Dallas and have a cooking school. I see cooking school in my future.

Every day is a new day in Cortona and I can't wait to go to the piazzas and see whom I shall meet today!

# Pietrotelli d' Italia

Peter, Pietro or Pietrotelli are the names he told me to call him.

Yesterday, Saturday, must have been my bewitching day. I was having cappuccino in the piazza; a man walked by several times, a beautiful man. When he walked by the third time and smiled, I did something that I have done, surely since birth, something I do without meaning to or thinking about, it is as natural as breathing to me, I winked. He winked back, I am sure he thought it was an invitation (may have been) on my part for him to stop and talk to me. He asked if he could join me and I said yes. Pietro does not speak much English and I little Italian, but eyes are a great vehicle for communication.

We introduced ourselves and began somewhat of a conversation. Pietro was looking very intently at me, so much so that I was becoming a bit intimidated. He reached across the table, put his fingertips on my cheeks and said, "You do not have a simple face, you have the most beautiful eyes and I am swimming in them."

I think he meant drowning in them, but hey, I was drowning myself. I ask him if he was trying to seduce me?

He said, "Seduce, seduce, I do not know this word, *che cosa?*"

I took my purse dictionary out and looked up the word seduce, it was not there.

I said, "Sort of like *amore* to mi."

He said, "Ah, *si, si mi* seduce you, *mi desiree maka perfecto* love a *tu*!"

Well okay then!

Pietro looks like a French *artista*, he has long black hair streaked with gray hair, and gorgeous green eyes. He does not look *Italiano*. At over six feet, and about 200 lbs., he is one very beautiful man. We shared prosecco and he told me his brother's wedding was at five today at Lago Trasimeno and would I be so kind as to join him. I told him I could not join him. Can you just see me at a large Italian wedding, with all *Italian's*, me not knowing anyone or speaking the language? *Impossibile*! He told me he understood but could he have an appointment with me *domani?* He was still looking intently in my eyes and must have caught my not understanding. I was thinking I misunderstood him and he thought I was selling something, or maybe he was and we needed an appointment.

He kissed my cheek and said, "I think in America you say data."

Oh, a date! The e's in italian are pronounced a, so date would translate to data!

I, of course, said, *"Va bene."* When I actually meant *molto bene!* My very first date in Italy.

I had a beauty shop appointment but told him I would meet him at il bar at three *domani.* He stood up, he took my hand and kissed it. He's got me!

After having my hair done, I stopped at my favorite Brazilian *ristorante* for lunch. I had just sat down when Peter and Rocco came walking up. Peter is an American from Virginia, and Rocco from New York City. I had met them both several days ago.

They said, *"Ciao,* can we join you for lunch?"

Americans may not speak to one another while in America but in Cortona we have that common bond being Americans and love to swap our stories about Cortona or Italy or Europe.

Rocco is married to Rahppipan from Thailand. Rocco is 54 and Rahppi is 30, they have been married for a year and are expecting their first child in October. Now Peter's story is fairly rich too. He is a physiologist and has one patient, a 47-year-old man named Jeff. Jeff's wealthy parents pay for the villa in Tuscany, the car, all of the bills and expenses and trips for Peter to care for Jeff. Not a bad gig! Peter says that Jeff is wonderful and easy to care for and to travel with. At this point I had not met Jeffery but once I did, I knew I had a friend for life.

The four of them were going to Castiglion Fiorentino for the evening for the *Sagra della Pastasciutta* festival and would I like to join them? There would be food and dancing and great fun.

I said sure and we arranged to meet at Piazza Gabernelli at 5:45. While waiting for Peter and his entourage at Piazza Gabernelli, I met a man and we chatted about the beautiful vista of the valley from our high point in Cortona. He asked if I had been to the top of the mountain to see the view; I had not. He offered to meet me at 2:00 the next day to take me to the top and have Sunday brunch. I explained to him that I was agreeable to do that but I had an appointment at three and must be *finito* by that time. My third date was set.

I said ciao to Luciano and got in the car with my group, and Peter (3) for the evening. Castiglion Fiorentino is about a 15 minute drive from Cortona. The crowd was very large, as the Italianos love their festivals and all *communialities* join the fun.

We ate from 7:30 until 9:30 and the dancing began. Peter is a great dancer and I really enjoyed dancing with him. I loved the company of all the new friends I had met. I was in heaven! It was well after two when I got home but it was a fabulous night.

The next day I was a wreck; too much wine, too much food and not enough sleep. I finally managed to roll out of bed. Upon awakening, I realized I had not even made my bed the night before. I had washed clothes early yesterday, including my sheets, and hung them on my suspended clothesline. When I got in last night, I was just too tired, so I laid one comforter on the bed and covered with the other one. I can see how Picasso ended up sleeping on a grass mat in the corner of a room.

We get too much into our dreams of life and the essentials become less important, or in Picasso's case not important in the least!

I crawled out of bed, made enough espresso for me to wake up and headed for the bathroom for that shower that takes an hour. Finally ready, I walked to the piazza for a cappuccino and still had time to go to the Internet Point to check my e-mail before meeting Luciano.

Entering the Internet Point, a man stopped me and asked, "If I was going to use the Internet (in Italian)?"

I said *"si"* and we started chatting about why I was here in Cortona, for how long, and where I lived.

When I came out of the Internet Point, he was waiting and asked if he could buy me a drink. I told him that would be okay but I only had a few minutes as I had an appointment soon.

His name is Angiolo, he lives in Cortona and his *papà e mamma* were the original owners of the real Bramasole (from *Under the Tuscan Sun*). At least that is what I think he said, in my limited knowledge of the Italian language. Later, I learned that was not what he said at all . . . of well, I was just learning Italian! We had a wonderful chat over coffee. Angiolo is maybe 56, probably more the type I should be dating, wealthy, very educated and nice. He just does not have that edge, that mystique that I love in a man. Anyway, he asked me to lunch and to go on a tour of Bromasola for Monday. I told him I was busy on Monday but could go with him on Tuesday. Tuesday we would be meeting at 9:00 having cappuccino, a tour and then lunch. He left in his BMW. What a big car to have in Cortona.

He lives in one of the Palaces (the real thing from the 13c) at the bottom of a street off of the Piazza.

Angiolo *is very* interesting and told me so much about Cortona and Tuscany that when it was time for me to leave for my next date, I really did not want to go.

My date with Luciano was limp. He does not speak enough English for me to follow and there is no edge, no mystique, no chemistry, no sing-song. I made the date as short as politeness was allowed, said ciao and was on my way to my real date, Pietrotilli! The date I had been dreaming of *mio bellissimo artista*!

# Market Day In Cortona
### "eat tomatoes"

My first Saturday in Cortona, I woke up at nine and went to the Piazza della Republica for my morning coffee. The piazza was full of people; there were hundreds of people slowly making their way through the piazza. I thought maybe everyone was evacuating the city. What with not being able to get a phone, all TV channels being in Italian, not being able to read a paper, I could have missed something about a war going on, or a deadly virus heading our way forcing all people to leave Italy.

The crowd forced me to move, ever so slowly, along with them. The crowd was moving toward the second piazza, Piazza Signorelli. As we approached Piazza Signorelli, I realized what the fuss was about. It was Market Day in Cortona.

I had never been to a market in Italy. I didn't even know how they could possibly get all of their wares into the city and set up in the Piazza. I was wondering what time it had started and how much I had missed. There were clothes, shoes, housewares, materials, jewelry and food and people on every square inch of the piazza. The crowd was so dense I couldn't even get close enough to see what things looked like much less what the prices were. What fun!

I though it might be a good idea for me to go back to Via Nazionale and have breakfast until the crowd thinned out, then I could come back and spend some serious time looking and shopping. I spent about thirty minutes forcing my way through a crowd going in the opposite direction. I swear I was pushed, pulled and pinched for doing so. It finally came to me that maybe I would be better off going with the flow of the crowd, making a circle through the piazza and entering the other piazza from the back. I eventually made my destination and was pleased I had survived in one piece.

There were no people at Caffé degli Artisti; I was all alone and happy about being out of the crowd. I drank two cappuccinos and ate my breakfast in peace. It took me some time to relax from being pushed and prodded.

Now, I had worked up the courage to go back and do some shopping. As I entered the piazza, there were just a few people; it was back to normal. I thought, wow, I have timed this perfectly and I do not have to fight the crowd. I turned the corner to Piazza Signorelli and it was gone. Market day in Cortona was over. How could that be, I had missed all of the shopping. They were loading up their wares and leaving town. I was so disappointed.

Okay, I thought, now that I know Cortona has market day on Saturday, I could make the perfect preparations for next Saturday. I would get up early and be one of the first on the Piazza and all of the prizes could be mine. I had the perfect plan.

The following Saturday I set my alarm, got up and was ready for the piazza and market day in Cortona. I left my apartment as excited as a kid at Christmas and headed out to shop. I went directly to the piazza and my timing could not have been better, I was right with the first wave of shoppers.

It was great, I was going from bin to bin. I wanted to see everything they had before I bought, you know, to make sure I was getting the very best prices. I ended up at the food center. All of the fresh fruits and vegetables made me want to cook. I had really been missing my fruits and vegetables. Here you eat mostly pasta and meat but I wasn't getting the fruits and vegetables and was craving them.

I could just imagine the aromas coming from my apartment cooking fresh vegetables. My dinner was decided, all fresh vegetables and fresh fruits for dinner . . . yum!

I was standing at a large bin, the crowds had arrived but I was at the front. These were the best looking vegetables I had ever seen and my mouth was watering. There were green beans, zucchini, tomatoes, potatoes, lettuce and every other kind of vegetable you could imagine. I reached in for the kill. I had to lean over, barely being able to reach, but I did; I had the prettiest tomato in my hand when all of a sudden out of nowhere my hand was slapped. Not only did she slap my hand she started screaming at me.

"STOP! STOP! DON'T TOUCH MY VEGETABLES!"

Holy cow, has the world gone mad! Don't touch my vegetables, indeed!

There are no words to say how embarrassed I was. I just fought my way out of the crowd and with my head down, I returned to my apartment. I'm not having fresh vegetables for dinner!

Having to summon much courage and determination, I decided to make a third attempt at market day in Cortona. I now know the rules (don't touch my vegetables) and the time I have to be there. I am prepared and I have even purchased a basket which to carry my fruits and vegetables in. I am ready!

I am happy and I am shopping. I have my basket about half full when I am overcome with an aroma from my basket. This was the sweetest aroma , it made my mouth water. I looked in my basket, started lifting things out and sniffing them. It was the tomatoes that had that sweet aroma.

I wondered how a tomato could have a sweet aroma. Back home I detest buying tomatoes, I think they have been frozen prior to shipping them to the stores. They have no flavor, no aroma and I would not buy them if not for the fact that it is hard to have a BLT without the T. And mozzarella caprese can't be without the tomato! I wanted to taste this tomato. And I wanted to taste it right at that moment. I did not want to go back to my apartment to taste the tomato, I wanted it now. So I picked that tomato out of my basket, thinking I would just take a small bite. Oh, my goddness, that was the finest tomato I have ever tasted. It was sweet, juicy and it was gone. I ate the whole thing and went back for another.

When in Cortona, eat tomatoes!

# Chiese di Cortona

Making the decision to visit all of the Churches in Cortona is no small feat, especially considering you must walk. Usually I find humor in everything I do and everything I write about. There is no humor in this story.

These are serious ancient architectural sites, religioun and art, invoking immense feelings and making you want to stay in each church for long periods of time.

I realized that within a two- week period I had been in more different churches than I had visited in my lifetime.

My visits so far have included 18 churches, the Duomo and Le Celle and I will spend the rest of my year in Cortona revisiting all of these beautiful churches. The Chiese di Cortona are museums in and of themselves. There is a wonderful book *Cortona city of art* which describes all of these churches in great detail. I have only mentioned a few details of the churches I have visited.

1. Church of S. Domenico is built outside the walls of Cortona and construction was completed in 1438. There is an altar piece by Lorenzo di Niccolò Gerini (XVc) showing The Coronation of the Virgin.

   Entering, on the right, is a Deposition by Baccio Bonetti, a Crucifix (1500s) on the first altar and a restored fresco (1400s).

2. Church of S. Agostino built 1256–1273. There are paintings of the Madonna of S.

Carlo Borromeo, St. John the Baptist and St. Anthony by Jacopo Chimenti (1554–1640).

3. Church of S. Benedetto, 1700's. It was built on the foundations of an Etruscan tower of 1306. Restructured in 1722 by Padri Scolopi, the shape changed from rectangular to oval.

   In the seventeenth century, the Florentine Taddeo Mazzi frescoed the vault with a representation of S. Guiseppe Calasanzio.

4. The Duomo standing on the remainder of the Etruscan and Medieval walls. A Romanesque parish church was built here around 1000, and altered in 1262 by Nicola Pisano. The construction of the present church was 1480–1507. In 1508 it was made a Cathedral. There are paintings attributable to the workshop of Signorelli and the Mosaic by Gino Severini of a Sacred Heart.

5. Church of the Gesù is opposite the Duomo via a stairway built in 1633. Built between 1498–1505, the Babtistry homes one of the rooms of Museo Diocesano.

6. Church of S. Filippo on Via Roma is a baroque building dating back to 1720. Built to the plan of the Cortonese architect Antonio Iannelli on a Latin cross plan. A painting (1745)
of St. Joseph and the Madonna by Venetian, Piazzetta is in the chapel and opposite is a picture by Cortonese, Domenico Venuti of S. Filippo Neri and The Madonna.

7. Church of S. Francesco, formerly an ancient Roman building, "Bagno de la Regina"(Queen's Bath). Later the Romans built baths there and perhaps also a pagan temple. There are works by Cortonesi, Mariotto Radi and Nicola Monti. Other works include B Florentine, Orazio Fidani, Andrea Commodi and Lodovico Cardi.

8. Church of S. Cristoforo situated on the top of the Poggio reached Via Berrettini, along the ancient Sienese walls. One of the oldest Churches of the town. A fourteenth century fresco, recently restored, depicting the Crucifixion, The Annunciation and The Ascension. Other arts include a Madonna and Child, Saint Elizabeth of Hungary, Saint Matthew, another Madonna and the Wedding of Saint Catherine, of 1530. Above the main altar is a painting of St. Christopher and Saint John, dated 1712 and signed by Pasquale Andrea Marini of Recanati.

9. Church of S. Niccolò is a small Gothic style church built in the fifteenth century. There is a bust of St. Francis in terracotta by the Cortonese, Diego Paoletti, 1955, and a Luca Signorelli's masterpiece depicting the Deposition of Jesus in the Sepulcher, 1510.
The Madonna and Child, a fresco by Sinorelli, was plastered over in

1768 and discovered in 1847. There is a water colour of S. Niccolò by Gino Severini.

10. Convent and Church of S. Chiara also in the Poggio area were built to a plan by Vasari,1581.Precious works include the painting in the lunette above the main altar which is by Lorenzo Berrettini, the gilded wooden altar is the work of Cortonese, Stefano Fabbrucci and two statues of St. Francis and St. Clare by his son Francesco Fabbrucci.

11. Church of SS Trinita was consecrated in February 1790 and dedicated to SS Trinita. Under the main altar lies the body of S. Felice, which was brought to Corona from the catacombs of Rome.

12. The Church of S. Caterina Da Siena, with adjoining convent, was built in 1426. In 1818, the Sisters of S. Francesco di Sales ran a Conservatory for girl boarders at S. Caterina. On the main altar there is a painting of the Madonna by Pietro Berrettini of 1659. Also a painting of S. Bernardino da Siena and others by Sebastiano Conca, of 1742, located in the chapel.

13. Church of S. Margherita, built in 1288. S. Margherita asked Guglielmino Bishop of Arezzo for authorization to re-build the oratory which had been built in 1217 but was refused permission. She obtained authorization 1290. After the death of the Saint, the community of Cortona built (1297–1304) a church dedicated to her, a plan by Giovanni Pisano and next to the existing oratory. The body of the Saint, urn of Saint Margaret, is visible in a casket on the main altar. The internal lining of the casket, made of solid silver, was designed by Pietro Berrettini (17c.). The casket top and side are of glass and in full view is her body. I have to tell you I was pretty freaked out by this and could not take my eyes off her while lighting a candle and saying a prayer. It was the first time I have ever seen someone who had been dead for 700 years.

There are paintings by Francesco Vanni, Pietro Gianotti, statues on the pilasters by Amalia Duprè sculpted between 1881–1884.

14. Church of S. Marco built in 1580 on the premises of the Compagnia della SS Trinità dei Laici. Arts by Andrea Commodi and Pietro

Berrettini and the baroque high altar is by Andrea Sellari. The lower church has a frescoed ceiling and 12 paintings on the walls depicting episodes of sacred history. In 1951, a beautiful mosaic of St. Mark, Patron of Cortona, by Gino Severini (1883–1966) was put on the outside façade in Via S. Margherita.

15. Church of Spirito Santo (XVIIc.) in the form of a Latin cross, was built between 1637–1669 to a plan by Filippo Berrettini. There are two statues on either side of the high altar by Francesco Fabbrucci of the Misericordia and Faith.

16. Church of Calcinaio, a masterpiece of Francesco di Giorgio Martini, dating back to1485–1513. It is the most beautiful Renaissance monument in Cortona. The stained-glass window is by Frenchman Guglielmo de Marcillat (1470–1529). A painting in one of the chapels of the Annunciation is by Cortonese, Tommaso Bernabei. There is also a Madonna by Jacone Fiorentino and an Immaculate Conception by the School of Signorelli in the chapels.

17. Church of S. Maria Nuova (XVIc), a late-Renaissance building in the form of a Greek cross, 1550 to a plan by Cristofanello. After his death the design was altered by Vasari. Paintings include, the Birth of the Madonna by Florentine, Allori and altarpieces Annunciation by Jacopo Chimenti and San Carlo Borromeo by Baccio da Barga.The stained-glass window of the Adoration of the Magi by Urbano Urbani, a pupil of Marcillat, in 1586.

18. Le Contesse (XIII c.) is situated in a beautilful garden with a stunning view of the valley. The convent, which belonged to the Sister Clarisse until 1237, adjoins the church which is dedicated to Our Lady and was built in 1718 to a design by the Cortonese Iannelli. During the Napoleonic period it was closed for several years and then restored and re-opened in 1804. At the end of the century it was re-structured and consecrated to the Madonna of Eternal Help. There is a terracotta Madonna delle Contesse, which came from the ancient monastery, made by a local craftsman, and a copy of the Byzantine-Cretan Madonna del Perpetuo Soccorso@ (the original is in the Church of St. Alfonso in Via Merulana in Rome) on the high altar.

19. The Cells (XVIIIc) Le Celle of Cortona, a stunning example of a Franciscan convent set on the slopes of Monte S. Egidio, over the Vignone Torrent. Saint Francis had it built in the early 1200's and Brother Elia, Beato Guido, S. Bonaventure and S. Antonio da Padova all lived there. The cell where the Saint stayed is still there. In the church the altarpiece on the high altar of the Madonna and Saints is by Giovanni Marracci (1637–1703). The convent is a fascinating place because of its unique position, and the silence that surrounds it, which creates a mystical atmosphere and also because of having sheltered the Poverello di Assisi (Mendicant of Assisi).

Many people come to pay tribute to St Francis' cell: a narrow quadrangular room, 1.80 by 2.50 m. and only 1.90 m. high. The Saint's bed is still preserved inside, as well as an old sand-glass and a copy of a painting of the Madonna and Child in front of which St. Francis used to pray. Through a small window in the wall facing the torrent you can see the place where the cell of Beato Guido was built, which was destroyed by a flood.

I will spend many days in these churches during my year in Cortona. Some I had already visited multiple times and always saw something I hadn't seen before.

# Un Mese a Cortona
## One Month in Cortona

I woke up this morning to a traffic jam at seven. I usually am awakened by Ms. Emberly between 7:30 and 8:00. Ms. Emberly is a pigeon that has taken a liking to me. She lights on the sill of my open window every morning. She started doing this about a week after I arrived. She lands and coos at me; if I don't respond she will just sit there nodding her funny little head until I wake up. I always say hello and talk to her and she sits there until I get out of bed. Ms. Emberly may actually be a dove, I don't know the difference.

This morning it was a traffic jam, with horns honking and people shouting. A traffic jam is not something we have in Cortona; not being able to see from my bedroom window, I stepped into my living room, looked out the window, an honest to goodness traffic jam in Cortona. It appears a large SUV, a *straniero* (foreigner) driving had gone up my street and upon reaching the top where one must take a sharp right or a sharp left, he could not make either turn.

A friend was trying to direct him, moving inch by inch, reversing and making more of those inch by inch moves. The people of Cortona are not used to traffic much less a traffic jam; now there were eight cars trying to get up my street, were not being patient and continued honking, getting out of their cars, yelling, on and on, like this was going to change the situation.

I went back to bed. When I walked in my bedroom, Ms. Emberly was sitting on my bed. As soon as she saw me she went to the window sill. How strange she would have come to my bed looking for me. Funny little bird!

I have also been living with a less desirable house guest for three days. At first I thought there was a large feather on my bathroom rug. It had been there for a couple of days reminding me that I really needed to find time to do some house cleaning. After I woke up for the second time today, I thought it would be a great morning to get the house cleaning over with before starting on more pleasurable things. I went into the bathroom with the intention of shaking my rug out the window the way all of the Cortonese women do (I love following their ways).

I noticed the feather was no longer on the rug and thought it must have blown away; yes, now I might not have to clean house after all. I stepped out of the bathroom into the center hall and there it was on the floor in the middle of the hall. When I reached down to pick it up, it moved. I turned on the light and got my glasses and, oh my gosh, it was the biggest scorpion I have ever seen.

This thing was at least five inches long with a stinger nearly as big. I put on a shoe and tried to tap it dead but no way; I had to stomp that sucker, two times. And then I couldn't pick it up to get it out of my apartment. I had to call Amy to come and take it away. No more house guest, thank you very much!

It caused me to strip my bed, move my furniture and take the throw covers off of my couches to make sure she didn't leave me any little presents in the way of babies. Yes, I have throw covers on both of my couches. That is also the Italian way.

It is hard to believe I have been here for a month. The time has gone by so fast and everyday has brought new pleasures. Pleasure in the things I do, the people I meet and the places I go. The weather changes have been on a slow pace of getting hotter. Everyday it has gotten a bit warmer to where it has reached the point of being really hot.

It is not that the temperature is greater than in Texas, actually it has just reached 90, but everything is of stone. The streets, the buildings and with the clay rooftops the heat just has a way of being very powerful. Unlike at home, you can't just run into your house or store or restaurant to cool off with air-conditioning. All these things we take for granted at home.

With the heat, I have decided it's time to take a trip to the mountains. I was headed north to the Dolomites then on to Lake Como. I have met some friends who live here and we all agree. It is time to go somewhere much cooler.

The Dolomites will be the first trip out of the Tuscan/Umbria region. Last week I went to Montepulciano for the olive oil festival. Montepulciano is known for its good local Vino Nobile wines. The Olive Oil Festival was an eye opener for really great olive oils selling for 225 E and smaller bottles of truffle oil for about the same cost.

The Duomo is a must to see when visiting. It was designed between 1592 and 1630 by Ippolito Scalza. Also, I think the most beautiful building is the Church of Madonna di San Biagio just on the outskirts of Montepuciano. Built of honey and cream colored travertine, it is Sangallo's masterpiece, a Renaissance gem with construction beginning in 1518.

If you like festivals, there can be one found in some town on almost a daily basis. Italians love to celebrate and their festivals have been traditions for hundreds of years. I usually go to one a week, enjoying the sites and activities from the surrounding towns.

Since the heat has moved in I have started doing the things in Cortona, so that when the heat becomes unbearable (for me) I can return to my apartment for a long siesta, not returning to the streets until 7 or 7:30. After dinner it has become habit to meet friends at The Fusion Bar and talk and drink Prosecco until midnight or later.

Massimo is the owner of the Fusion Bar and he and I have a system worked out. He tells me there is normally one village idiot per town but Cortona has about 20 and they are all after me.

If I go to the bar alone and someone sits down at my table, Massimo will come over and say, "Carlotta (what the Italians call me) SOS?"

If I say "*si*," he scoots the man or men off for me. Isn't that nice?

We all love the Fusion Bar, me especially; it takes me, momentarily, out of the 13c and back into the world I have left behind. The decor is strictly high-tech LA, with air-conditioning and great music. It is a very popular place in Cortona, but unlike its sister bars, it has none of the age or character.

My dating life has been staggering and I actually have to write down, on paper, the dates I have made in order to keep them straight and not (I have) double book. I usually have 3–5 dates in one day. I go, of course, on the normal dates: coffee, lunch, dinner, etc. But my dates also include: flower picking in the meadows, church and museum dates, lake dates and walking dates. It's a wild ride after being practically dateless for two years.

I have come to the conclusion that I am dating 13 percent of the available Cortona men. If the population is indeed 1600, half being men and 20 percent are single, separated or just available and I can date in two generations, my dates are between 42–61. With my dance card being continuously full, you would think, I am the only single American woman in Cortona, *oh that's right, I am*! I am not really the only single woman in Cortona but at times it feels that way. It occurred to me that in order to meet and date more men, I must begin the process of weeding some of my men out.

I have already picked the first to go with good reason; he bent over at lunch yesterday, and oh my goodness, the man was wearing a thong. I cannot possibly date a man who wears sexier underwear than me. I am still in my white jockey, granny panties. I do believe it is time to shop for more sexy undies.

# Mangiare, Vino and the Weather

You might wonder what the weather would have to do with eating and drinking *vino*. From the Cortonese point of view and totally from my point of view, everything!

We (Cortonese) for the most part do not have cars. In order to have a car, in the walls of Cortona, you must have a home for your car. We barely have a street (alley) much less a home for a car. Some of the wealthy Cortonese, living in the Palaces do have cars and homes for those cars. I am not one of them.

Most all of the existing residential buildings were originally built as Palaces occupied by the wealthy with large families and most times two to three generations (and the help) living in these palaces. Some of the once- palaces, closer to center city, have been made into apartment buildings such as where I live. There is an antique street just off the Piazza of the Duomo where the oldest houses of Cortona still exist.

If it rains in Cortona, being on a steep hill, all of the water runs, obviously, down hill into the low alleys and into the piazzas. An umbrella might keep the top of you dry but there is nothing that is going to keep the shoes or pants dry. That means, unless you cook at home, (I don't), you will get wet on the way to eat. I have and will continue to get wet in order to eat.

Now, if the rain continues, you cannot eat outside. We all prefer to eat outside. The restaurants in the piazza are one right after the other, or across from one another, so eating outside is like you are eating with 200 people. Everyone talks either about living here, visiting here or wanting to move here. There are continual salutes and the wine flows. Also, most Europeans smoke, but they have taken to the American point of view and made inside restaurants non-smoking! So, we all want outside tables.

It does not matter how hot it gets, we still want outside tables. Now the cold is another matter. I have not experienced the cold, the winter, but I am sure there will be no outside tables and the eating will be less joyous. I have become very accustomed to this eating with large, fun groups and I am sure I will miss this as winter approaches.

The population of course triples in the season, April through September, so the piazzas, anytime of day or night is active and the tables are full. The conversations are wonderful to be included in or to just to listen to. Everyone has a story and most of them about travel and always entertaining.

When I moved to Cortona, one of my first questions was "What is the population of Cortona?" Well no one really knows and they don't even worry about it. With some pushing and nudging I did come up with a number of around 1,600. The accuracy of that number is very questionable. I was having dinner one night with Amy and Giovanni (the tour guide) and Giovanni, just coming off a tour made mention that all Americans first question during a tour is, "What is the population of Cortona." He said it was such a silly question. "Who cares, what does it matter and if I gave them the information, what would they do with it!"

I am glad I didn't ask him the population of Cortona.

There are (to my count) 28 restaurants in the walls of Cortona. This includes *il ristoranti, la trattoria, l'osteria, la tavola calda and il bar.* That's many restaurants for a town the size of Cortona, so you can imagine most of the business is done and the incomes made during the tourist season.

It also surprised me (maybe not) to find that local prices and tourist prices are not the same in all restaurants. In one café, I am charged 1.80 E for a cappuccino and a croissant (where they consider me a local) where as in another I am charge 2 E for just a cappuccino. But at the same time, many of the *ristorantis* give you things for free all of the time.

Prosecco is my new favorite drink; I always have two around six, a couple of hours before dinner. Prosecco is like champagne but better. Don't ever say to an Italian that prosecco is like champagne, they will look at you like you are crazy and say, "The French make champagne, we make prosecco!" The local drink, of course, is *vino.* We are in Tuscany, the best *vinos* in Italia!

If you want the most economical wine, ask for the local open wine (not in bottles but served from pitchers) or *vino della casa*, ordered in *una bottiglia, mezza litro, or un quartino*. Or you can sample by the glass, *un bicchiere di vino*. Vintages are not very important in Italy. The weather is usually good and one year is generally as good as the other. White wines, however, are best when two years old at most, one year is even better. Chianti is of course the wine of Tuscany.

Tuscany's best wines include Brunello di Montalcino, Chianti Riserva, and Vino Nobile di Montepulciano.

Many Tuscan wine producers come from ancient noble families. The Ricasoli trace their association with wine making to 1141, the Frescobaldi to 1300. Antinori, one of the region's fine estates, has been in operation for over 600 years.

Most tourists select bottles of the best and most expensive *(caro)* wines from the wine menu. It really is not necessary to do that, the *vino della casa* are excellent wines, just not labeled, and Italians would never serve a bad *vino*! But we must splurge because these are some of the best wines of the world and always worth the price.

Food. Ah the food! Of course, like every city we visit, we have our favorite restaurants. I already have mine. I have not tried all of the eateries in Cortona, it will take me some time to do so, and some of the ones I have been to, I keep going back. I have to make myself go to different restaurants but some of my favorites keep capturing me with their wonderful dishes.

# Restaurants di Cortona

In planning my move to Cortona, I did two personal things, let my hair grow long and got down to a size four. Size four occupied my suitcases when it occurred to me that I might gain weight on pasta and pizza, so I threw in some size sixes.

After being in Cortona only two weeks, I had a great fear of going from a size 4 to a size 8, completely bypassing size 6.

The foods in Tuscany are superb and I found reasons to eat all day without the slightest notion of being hungry, I just love the foods!

Tuscany, however wonderful, is not known just for pasta and pizza. For breakfast there is Brioche, jam or custard (my personal favorite) filled buns. There is an array of antipasto that makes my mouth water. *Panzanella* is a salad of basil, tomatoes, parsley, garlic and oil soaked bread.

*Bruschetta* are slices of toasted breads with choices of toppings, olive paste, liver paste, tomato paste and anchovy paste. One of my favorite antipasto is the *Salame di Cinghiale*, wild boar, usually served with a variety of cheese, olives and breads.

The soups of the region are *Ribollita*, a thickened soup of cabbage, beans and vegetables or *Fagioli all'Uccelletto* (yum!) of white bean, vegetables, tomato sauce and sometimes hard toasted pieces of bread.

*Pappardelle alla Lepre* is a broad noodle with hare sauce. The chefs cook the hare in it's own blood which I preferred not to know.

Another region favorite (not of mine) is *Trippa alla Fiorentina* topped with tomato sauce and parmesan cheese. For the beef lovers, *Bistecca alla Fiorentina*, much like our porterhouse steaks, cooked on an open fire seasoned with oil and herbs. Each year in *Agosto*, Cortona has it's *bistecca* festival with large open grills filled with tender steaks. Wild Boar is in abundance; at night you can first hear then see the wild boar roaming the hillsides.

During my first visit to Cortona I was visiting the home of some friends I met from New Jersey. They had recently purchased a villa situated on the hills of Cortona. I had been invited for a light meal and wine which we enjoyed on their terrace overlooking the Le Celle and the valley. At nightfall, with the cool air, we moved inside for coffee and *vin santo*.

After only a short time indoors I heard a snorting sound and inquired as to what it could be. Our host told me to look outside. It was the wild boars, snorting and rooting for any food that may have been left. They are hunted animals so they tend to be shy and not aggressive. My favorite wild boar dish is *Scottiglia di Cinghiale*, boar chop. I also love the wild boar sausage with *patate fritte*.

Their cheese is, of course, Pecorino, made from sheep's milk. They eat Ricotta, made from sheep's milk, too, with olive oil which is the way I have always eaten it, but they also eat Ricotta with honey, very good.

Now my downfall, with many others, is dessert. *Panna Cotta* (cooked cream) with honey or caramel is my favorite but I think I have tried them all. *Castagne Ubriache*, chestnuts covered in red wine sauce served with baked custard or *Torta di Riso*, rice cakes with fruit sauce. For that afternoon sweet tooth or after dinner try the Panforte, a dense, hard cake spiced with cloves and cinnamon or *Ricciarelli* with ground almonds, candied orange peel and honey. I enjoy these with my afternoon espresso or *caffe macchiato*.

The Italians enjoy eating dinner late and lento. They begin with antipasto, first piatto (a pasta), sec (main course*), insalata* followed sometimes by dessert but generally *Cantucci*, a sweet cookie with *vin santo*. All of this is then followed by an espresso.

Like the Churches of Cortona (I think 28), there are as many restaurants, at least 28, but I am sure I have missed some tucked away or up high in the hills. In my two months in Cortona, I have only enjoyed 15 of these restaurants.

I have my very favorite but unlike many restaurants in my past, there has not been even one out of 15 that I would not return for another dining experience.

Last September, my first visit to Cortona, I had the pleasure of dining at the 'Osteria del Teatro' restaurant with Giovanni and Amy. It is a lovely restaurant, family owned and operated. The chef is one of the sons and the other son owns another restaurant, '*Taverna Pane e Vino*' in Piazza Signorelli.

We had started our dinner with *Antipasto della Casa* and I had ordered the pork tenderloin with truffle cream sauce. I felt sure it would be wild boar since this is a town classic dish. My mouth was watering!

We were visiting and having a great time, me learning some of the history of Cortona from Giovanni (the tour guide) when out of nowhere came the oddest sound I had ever heard. The screeching or whatever did not last long but my imagination ran wild wondering what it could be. No one reacted so I didn't want to bring it up, but I finally decided it sounded like a pig squealing. After deciding the sound my imagination leaped further and I got a mental visual of a pig (or wild boar) hanging from the rafter in the kitchen and being butchered. Along with this mental picture I imagined a bucket under the pig to drain the blood, since I had just learned they use pig blood (and cows) for many of the dishes. My pork tenderloin was not sounding very appetizing anymore!

I tried to just sit there, not react, calm down and certainly not throw up. Breathe deeply and slowly. Okay, I can manage this, I think! About the time I had calmed myself and no longer feeling as though I was going to lose my food, the screeching came again, only this time it was in the dining room, right behind me. You can be sure I thought the darn thing had gotten loose and was running around in the dinning room with it's throat slit! Nightmare, but of course I had to turn around and look. Oh, my goodness, it's a woman, the waitress (chef's girlfriend) and that screeching noise was her laughing. I became hysterical at this and told Amy and Giovanni what I had been imagining.

Of course, Giovanni, being the way he is, had to inform everyone in the restaurant and I was the joke of the night. But that's okay, better than a pig.

The best part, and I could not have dreamed it to come true, that only several months later I would be living on the same street as this lovely restaurant (almost directly across the street) with this great girl, whom I adore, and almost nightly falling asleep to the sound of the squealing of the wild boar.

# Contessa Carlotta
## Countess of Garda

The Italians have changed my name to Carlotta and I have added Contessa; now I am Contessa Carlotta!

I just returned from my first road trip (by car) to the northern parts of Italy. It had gotten so hot in Cortona that several of us decided to head to the Dolomites.

The first day we drove to Lake Garda with the intention of exploring parts of the lake and continuing on to the Dolomites but I "fell in love" and we stayed for two days.

Lake Garda and the surrounding towns are magical, with sailboats, blue water and the mountains rising in the background. Lake Garda is an island of scenery without compare, a Mediterranean spot immersed in the savage grandeur of the Alpine mountains.

The town of Sirmione, with its Scaligero Castle, is an impressive fortress, standing like a sentinel to the antique township giving the town a truly medieval aspect. The Signori Della Scala, with the Castle and the high walls and towers which once ringed the entire Village, are the works of the Lords Della Scala. It is said that Cangrande was responsible for the transformation of the old Castle of Sirmione into the present fortress. The Castle today is reached, after passing through the barbican which gives access to the town, over a drawbridge facing towards the square. Sirmione is an island connected to land by the drawbridge.

Gardone Riviera is one of the most elegant and beautiful areas of the lake for the variety and magnificence of its vegetation due to the mildness of the climate. It is a famous, international sojourn station lying among bright hills, large gardens, villas and sumptuous hotels.

Salo is one of the most important commercial and tourist centres of the west Riviera of Garda. It lies in a wide, pleasant gulf on the slopes of mount S. Bartolomeo. From the neighboring hills you can see rich villas and olive gardens.

Desenzano del Garda is a picturesque small town, situated on the south part of the lake on the famous gulf, has got the widest and best equipped port of Garda and the ancient characteristic small port surrounded by buildings on three sides.

But the town of Garda is where I fell in love and where we stayed during the nights. We would tour the towns during the day, returning to Garda by nightfall. Garda lies in the middle of a wonderful gulf with very curved banks and is protected by the slopes of Mount Blado and by the fortress and the moraine heights.

On the second evening at Garda the group, except for me, wanted to take the boat across the lake for dinner with plans of returning late. I told them to go ahead but I was staying behind. I wanted some alone time, a nice silent dinner and a bath in my room. I bid them all a goodnight and headed for my hotel room. Having only a shower in my apartment in Cortona, a bathtub is my everything. I was headed for a long bubble bath and a bottle of prosecco.

Dressed and feeling wonderful, I found myself at a charming restaurant, relaxing and hungry. I ordered a bottle of red Terre di Franciacorta wine and began reviewing the menu. Scanning the menu I realized I was in the area known for Cotoletta all Milanese, an authentic Milanese veal cutlet of tender veal loin. The veal is covered with breadcrumbs and then lightly fried in butter. Yum!

While waiting for my wine and to order, I looked around the restaurant and discovered the total beauty of the dome-shaped room with its immense center core and surrounding balcony with seating. I loved the red linen tablecloths and high backed gold brocade chairs.

I was admiring all of this grandeur when my waiter arrived with a bottle of champagne (oh no, I am in Italy, why is he serving me champagne?). I told him I had ordered wine, there must be a mistake. He said it was compliments of the gentleman seated at the corner table on the balcony. I looked toward the balcony, seeing a lone gentleman diner, with an entourage of three men sitting off to the side. I nodded my appreciation for the champagne and wondered to myself why he had sent it to me. Only a moment later, the matre'd appeared at my table with a card on a silver tray. I took the card and it was a request, from my admirer, to join me. I agreed, loving the adventure and the opportunity to meet a new person. He came to my table and introduced himself as the Count of Garda! Oh my gosh, I was meeting a Count.

What a fabulous man, not on a romantic level but certainly on an adventurous level. And I had visited, just that very day, his palace. Conversation was great and he shared with me so many wonderful stories of Garda. As the champagne set in so did my need to express myself.

I told him I had visited the palace and even with its immense beauty and acres and acres of gardens I had felt a certain sadness engulfing the palace. I told him of my sitting on the bench in his gardens imagining me bringing the palace to full life and happiness. That I would have lush flowers, of every color, replacing the now only green gardens and that the motor court would be filled with cars for grand parties and the two medieval gates of the fencing walls would be standing open. The gothic Venetian Palace porches and terraces would be filled with dancers and artists with easels capturing their every move. And inside the immense entry hall with the grand staircase he would be awaiting my descent to escort me into the ballroom for the first dance of the evening. The dining hall would be set for dinner parties of no less than 300 guests and he would become the grand count, the count for the people of Garda and I, I would be Contessa Carlotta, the Countess of Garda. He thought this to be great fun and I knew I had a friend in him forever. I love Garda!

# The Dolomites

We all make a great mistake when traveling. Time limits restrict us through-out our lives but especially in travel. Planning vacations and travel have become like having a job where there is never enough time. We tend, like our lives, to overbook, not allowing enough time and missing so much in our travels. We return home from exhausting trips and try to recapture, through pictures we have taken while on vacation, the beauty we were too busy to really enjoy. Stop, please, and smell the roses!

Living my life today, I have no agenda and have the luxury of deciding on a destination without time limits. Thank you my lord! Deciding the Dolomites was the destination, I was off on a wonderful excursion.

I have shared the story with you of finding myself at Lake Garda and wanting to stay, which of course I did, but finally I left Garda and continued the trip to the Dolomites.

Those who have not seen the Dolomites at least once in their lives cannot say they are true lovers of the mountains. For while every mountain landscape is beautiful in its own way, the Dolomites are like precious stones of an old family ring—they have that something extra. Perhaps it's their position in the heart of Europe, or else the pink hues of the sunsets. They have even named these glorious sunsets, a special word in Italian with Ladin origins, "enrosadira," which refers to the gradual pink hue that blends into purple which the walls of the Dolomites take on at dusk. I visited during the time of flowers blooming, wild flowers of every color, size and shape.

Taking a cable car to a very high peak, I found myself soaring high above the towns with a breathtaking view of below. At that peak we walked a five mile trail, slowly slanting upwards reaching into the clouds. It was heavenly walking through the fields and fields of beautiful flowers.

We enjoyed lunch on a terrace with views of Cavalese and views toward the Alps Cermis. From there we took the ski lift to an even higher peak for more hiking and picture taking. The air is so clean and fresh, I felt I could have walked for hours.

In the towns you feel as though you are no longer in Italy but have somehow arrived in either Austria or Bavarian, Germany. Many of the people speak German, the foods are more German, as is the architecture. But I was in Italy. One of the Dolomites' largest populations is the Ladin people, who number over 30,000. Their name is derived from the language spoken in these parts, a Romance language which is a descendant of Latin.

To protect the tradition of this people, an association was established in 1905 called "Union Ladina," which after the Second World War became the "Union di Ladins." The individual Unions of the various valleys are united under the "Union Generala di Ladins della Dolomites."

The peaks of the Dolomites are sprinkled with farm houses, small towns or villages and castles with grand defense moats. Realizing defense was at one time a priority, I did not understand the need. The castles are situated on peaks so high, actually rock ledges, I would have thought it impossible to ever reach.

The vineyards slope upward on the mountains at steep angles making harvesting very difficult. I want to be there at harvest time, I think late September, and watch it take place.

An open-air museum, a project supported by the European Union has allowed for the reconstruction of tunnels, barracks, trenches and encampments that help us understand the conditions the "Alpini" regiments and their Austrian counterparts had to fight under. If you take the cable car to the top of mount Lagazuoi, you can walk down to the Flazarego Pass along a route displaying authentic relics dating back almost a hundred years.

I had the pleasure of staying at the Hotel Lersc in Ortisei-St. Ulrich with its family atmosphere and surrounded by greenery. It is located a short walk from the Seceda cable-car that connects to the ski-lifts to Sella Ronda. I had a beautiful room with a balcony overlooking the valley and the Dolomites and a bathtub. This is, as many are, a family owned hotel. Included with our rooms were breakfast and dinner. The home-cooked cuisine was excellent and consisted of delicious national dishes.

When visiting Europe, please make time, I mean real time, to spend days in the Dolomites.

# Lake Como

Lake Como, known as Lario, is situated north of Milano and is considered the Riviera of Italy with immense villas housing some of the wealthiest people of the world. The lake is in the shape of an upside down Y, and at the top part of the V is the town of Bellagio, my favorite town. It is the third largest lake in Italy. The legs of the upside down Y divide the lake, with the west portion a continuation of Lake Como (Lago di Como) and the east portion being Lake Lecco (Lago di Lecco).

There is a narrow and winding road taking you around the entire lake. The vistas are magnificent and the homes, villas and castles are the most beautiful of any place I have visited in Italy.

We began our journey around the lake at the town of Como, located at the bottom of the V on the Lake Como's western tip. The Como shore is the most developed with restaurants and hotels, with a scenic road that follows the ancient Strada Regina, lined with elegant villas and aristocratic gardens. Construction of Como's Duomo began in 1396 and ended in 1740 with a huge dome. Next to the Duomo is the elegant thirteenth c Broletto, the old town hall.

Following the road from Como it is a short trip to Cernobbio where there is a famous hotel in the sixteenth c Villa d'Este surrounded by beautiful landscaped garden with many fountains, once hosts to the Duke of Windsor and Mrs. Simpson.

In Tremezzo is Villa Carlotta which was a wedding gift for Carlotta of Prussia in 1843. Inside there is a copy of Canova's Cupid and Psyche. I think this should be my villa. It was built in the eighteenth c by Marchese Giorgio Clerici.

Bellagio with its position at the junction of the arms of the lake and the spectacular view from the Spartivento point make this one of the most popular spots on Lake Como. Be patient, as the road, with its twists and turns and hairpin bends, from Como to Bellagio, while not a great distance, takes two hours or more to arrive. Plan on enough time to stop often for picture taking and enjoying the available tours, one could spend all day on this tiny roadway. Bellagio is one of the most famous tourist resorts around the lake.

Situated at the tip of the promontory that divides Lake Como into the two branches of Como and Lecco. This town boasts famous villas with luxurious gardens. Along the arched promenade are elegant cafés, bars and shops. Villa Serbelloni is perched way above, it is part of the Rockefeller foundation and hosts many cultural meetings.

From Bellagio, you can take ferries to Menaggio or Varenna, both beautiful places to visit. The name Menaggio supposedly derives from two Indo-European words, men (mountain) and uigg (water), referring to the mouth of the Sanagr river on which the town lies. Menaggio is the leading commercial centre and a very popular tourist resort, especially popular with British visitors. Don't be put off by the ferry, and be sure to make this one of your stops when visiting Lake Como.

Varenna is a splendid village (also by ferry from Bellagio) of ancient Roman origin, with a perfectly intact medieval layout. In the town centre, fourteenth c San Giorgio has an altarpiece by Pietro Brentani (1467), while the Santa Marta houses the parish art gallery. Varenna is famous for Villa Monaster, built over a Cistercian monastery. Some of the paths in this village, one of the best preserved on the lake, consists of steps and raised boardwalks perched over the water. What a splendid dining experience. I have decided my next trip to Lake Como will be by train and I will hire a driver for a week. It may even take longer than a week to tour all of the beautiful villages and to get to know the culture and the local foods. The fish from the lake is divine.

# Travel and Transportation in Italy

I have never ridden a bus. Well, maybe I have been on buses but only in other countries, in a group with planned activities. I have never had to purchase a ticket, figure out a bus schedule or learn where to get on and off a bus. Here I was in Italy, knowing I was going to have to learn all of this, but assuming I would have time to acclimate and learn *lento* (slow).

Because of *mal di denti*, I didn't have time for lento; I had to learn the fast and hard way. The English speaking dentist I found happened to be six towns away. To make matters even more difficult he was in Umbria and I was in Tuscany. From the Italian point of view Umbria and Tuscany are somewhat like different countries.

The Tuscany buses stop in Terontola. Terontola is the last town in Tuscany and the next closest town; 12 miles away is the first town in Umbria. Your choices once in Terontola to get to Castiglion del Lago (where my dentist is located) is to either take a taxi, 15 e, or a train for 1.80 e. I had called the dentist and made an appointment for 11 am thinking this would give me more than enough time to go the 40 miles by bus and whatever other transportation I decided to take. I arrived at the bus station in Cortona at 8 am, the bus was due to arrive at 8:05.

There is this strange little old man that is always either at the bus stop, or as I found out later, he may actually be on any given bus at any given time. He thinks he works for the bus department. He checks people's tickets, tries to tell them where to get off, asks questions about their opinions of the bus service and so on. This man is well into his late seventies and does not work for the bus department, maybe he used to, and it is generally thought that he is crazy but harmless. I guess he thinks his pension check is a pay check because rain or shine he is at the bus stop seven days a week. The bus was exact, 8:05 it arrived and I boarded the bus prepared to buy my ticket. I asked the bus driver, *"Quanto costa il biglietto?"*

He said in his polite English, "You must buy your ticket at *il tabaccaio.*"

Okay, I was not getting on this bus. I walked back into town to the *tabaccaio* and bought a bus ticket to Camucia, thinking I would take the train to Terontola and a taxi on to Castiglione del Lago.

I got back to the bus stop at 8:25 and according to the bus schedule I had, the next bus to the train station in Camucia was not until 9:05 but at 8:35 another bus showed up that said Camucia so on I went with ticket in hand. Upon boarding the bus I watched as people placed their tickets into the yellow machines and had them stamped so I did the same.

The bus got down the hill to Camucia and made it's first stop, which was not the train station, so I stayed on the bus preparing to get off at the next stop, the train station. We rode on for a while and then I saw a Camucia sign with a red line going through it, which meant we were leaving Camucia. Oh no, it did not stop at the train station. I was wondering where in the world I was headed.

I walked up to the front of the bus trying to get the bus driver's attention. He was talking on his cell phone and just ignored me.

I got to say one of my favorite words, *"Basta! Basta!"* still thinking basta meant to stop.

That got his attention and he asked me, "What is wrong?"

I said, "I was supposed to get off at the train station in Camucia!"

He said, "This bus does not go to the train station."

"Obviously, but now I have to get off."

We were well outside of Camucia; again I said, "Obviously, but I have to get off and where does this bus go?"

"We are headed for Arezzo (about 50 miles in the wrong direction). He then told me that we were not at a bus stop!"

Again I said, "Obviously, but I still need to get off of this bus!"

He finally stopped the bus, told me it was a very long walk to the train station. Obviously!

Indeed, it was a long walk to the train station and took me 30 minutes to make the walk but I finally had arrived. I went into the terminal and asked where to buy a ticket and was told to go across the street to the bar. I went into the bar, purchased my ticket and asked what time the train would be leaving for Castiglion del Lago. He informed me that it was leaving now. I ran across the street, a man saw me and I guess asked the conductor to wait; he did and I was grateful.

At this point I was a bit worried about making my 11 am appointment but I decided to just relax and have a cigarette, calm my nerves and I would get there when I got there.

I leaned back in my chair and lit a cigarette and had just begun to relax when the ticket guy came by to check my ticket. I think he told me that there would be a fine for not getting my ticket stamped by yet another little machine at the terminal and something about my smoking.

I told him, "*Mi dispiace, io parlo poco Italiano.*"

He waved his hand and just went on, not giving me a fine. *Grazie!* I assumed at this point that I was in a nonsmoking car on the train but no one else was in the car so I continued to smoke. I found out much later, way after this trip and many other train travels, that all of the trains in Italy are now nonsmoking and carry a hefty fine.

I got off the train in Terontola and went to the bar to inquire about a taxi. The bar owner told me the taxis were on strike today. I asked him how to get to Castiglion del Lago and was informed my only choice was to take another train. I purchased a train ticket from him, went back to the train station and found the machine, stamped my ticket and waited for the next train, hopefully the right train.

I finally made it to Castiglion del Lago, got off the train, which is almost out of town and certainly a long way away from town center. Town center was straight up a hill and I knew I was in for another very long walk. I arrived at the dentist an hour and a half later than my scheduled appointment but when I described what I had been through, he took me right in. Since that experience with the train and the bus, I have not become an expert but I am getting much better. I am still learning the times and because of one problem I had in my travels, I now check the bus schedule to the connecting train schedule and vice versa.

I went to Pienza, first by bus to Camucia, then by train and another bus. I fell in love with the town. I didn't get there until late morning. I walked and shopped and stopped for a late lunch. I had a great two hour lunch and then continued to walk and take pictures and lost track of time. I decided it was time to make the trip home but when I got to the bus station the last bus of the day had already left so like it or not I was spending the night in Pienza. Well that was all well and good but the fact was that there were no available hotels. I ended up spending the night in il tabaccaio. The owner was very nice, made me cappuccino, gave me cigarettes and even offered for his wife to come pick me up and take me to their home for the night. I declined and caught the 7 am bus home.

My other little travel mistake got me into Camucia by train one night, but the bus service to Cortona was closed for the night. Now Cortona, like many of the hill towns, has a serious curvy road up the hill. It looks like a big snake with s-turns, up and down turns and u-turns. It is about a ten minute drive but a two hour walk. I knew I could never make this walk but I had no choice. I have two fears about walking in Italy. The first being dogs. Italians love dogs and they are in abundance. The Italians let their dogs run free and as most of them are lovable, I knew with my luck I would encounter the mean ones. My other fear is this little viper they have; it is the color of dirt, not very long, small and very deadly.

I stood at the base of the hill, all of my fears going through my head telling myself, "buck up girl, you can do this." Off I took for my long journey uphill. I had only walked for about 20 minutes when a car pulled over. I thought, oh no, now I get some idiot to harm me, a thought that had not entered my head until now. The driver turned out to be someone from Cortona that I knew and was offering me a ride. Yes!

The driver was Gino. I met Gino the first day in Cortona and he actually chased me around town for weeks, trying for my attentions. I finally had to tell him that there was to be no *romantico* between us. From that point on, Gino just stopped talking to me. When I would see him in the Piazza, he would just nod but never speak. Oh well.

Gino drove me to the top of the hill and dropped me off. I told him how thankful I was and how much I appreciated the ride.

He said, "Now you have accepted from me, now there will be *romantico!*"

"No Gino, I am going to marry the Count of Lago de Garda and become Contessa Carlotta, Countess of Lake Garda. *Ciao, Ciao!*"

Even with all of my learning experiences traveling on the buses and trains of Italy, it is two of my many pleasures in Italy. I get to enjoy seeing the fields and fields (acres and acres) of the biggest and most beautiful sunflowers. They are as tall as me and the blooms are as large as my face. I was not aware that the sunflowers follow the sun. In the mornings they are standing tall and proud, the best time to photograph them, where as in the evenings they turn and hang their heads down, still very pretty. You will find these fields of yellow sunflowers next to fields and fields of the reddest poppies, and following the poppies the fields and fields of beautiful and so blue, the lilacs. I often thought the post cards of the flowers were enhanced but they are not. The flowers are majestic!

Obviously, the other mode of transportation in Italy is the car. Known as the macchina, most Italians have them and do drive them. Most of the tourists rent them and drive them across the country. The cost is caro with the tolls and the high cost of insurance. Amy had driven me around so many times, and I felt I needed to buy gas. We had gone to the COOP and I noticed her tank was on empty, so I told her to pull over and I would fill her car up with gas. She did pull into the station but told me that no, I did not want to fill the car up. She said her and Giovanni usually stopped and bought 20–25 euro at a time. I said that is ridiculous, I will fill it up.

I had no idea what a costly endeavor this was to be and was thankful I had money (a lot) with me. She drives a VW, same size tank I have in my Mercedes. It cost me $30 at home to fill up my car, which I (along with the rest of the Americans I know) constantly complain about. The attendant started pumping the gas. I told Amy we no longer had attendants at home, we were on our own for pumping gas and wondered aloud how the stations could afford to hire people to pump gas. I also noticed the gas prices were 1.68 euro and thought to myself how gas could be cheaper then the prices in the states. Well folks, that's the price per liter. This precious tank of gas cost 96 euro's which is about 120 dollars. I will never again complain about the price of gas in the states!

# Orvieto

Terrell came for a visit. She had been in Turkey for two weeks and decided to include a week in Italy in her travels. Terrell is an ex-sister-in-law and Amy's aunt.

Terrell works in a travel book store in Seattle and writes for their travel web-site. She fell in love with Turkey and enjoys the company of a tour guide there. Each year, she travels with this tour guide to different places in Turkey and writes about her experiences.

Terrell spent a year with a host family in Italy after high school and before university. She had fallen in love with the "host family" son while in Italy, and even though he was crazy to marry her, she was too young.

Making the most of a mere one week visit in Tuscany cannot do Tuscany justice but we did our best. She spent time in Rome, Camucia, Cortona, Siena and Orvieto. Neither of us had visited Orvieto and decided to spend an entire day there.

From Cortona, we took the bus to Camucia and then a train to the base of the hill of Orvieta, about an hour trip going south towards Roma. At the base, you take the Funicular, much like a cable car on tracks, up to the top and into the world of Orvieto.

Due to its position, its Etruscan antiquities, the partly medieval appearance of its street and above all its famous Cathedral, a jewel of Gothic art, Orvieto is one of the most fascinating towns in Italy. Orvieto is surrounded by an extensive region of hill country, from which fine views can be enjoyed of the numerous farmsteads scattered over the hilltops and of a few small villages consisting of ancient inhabited centres.

The whole area bases its prosperity not only on tourism, which has been developed considerably, but on a flourishing agriculture. Apart from olive oil, this is dominated by viticulture, from which the famous "Wine of Orvieto" is produced. Orvieto is not a large città and I am amazed by its Duomo, being one of the grandest of all of the hilltop towns I have visited, comparable, and even more beautiful than, the Duomo in Siena. It took three centuries to complete the building of this Duomo. A Sienese architect and sculptor, Lorenzo Maitani, delighted the citizens of Orvieto with his coloured design for a triple-gabled façade to the new church.

Terrell and I took in all of the sites, visiting the churches and museums and shopping. We had local cuisine for lunch. We shopped in the local ceramic Shoppes. The art of pottery in Orvieto dates back to the thirteenth C, the period in which the first products of Umbrian ceramics were identifiable. The pottery style is called "archaic" from Orvieto's previous culture, from that of etruria onwards, combined with intrusive elements of hispano-moresque pottery. I had a great time watching the local potters making their ceramics.

I had not seen all of Orvieto but it was time to catch the train. I decided I would return for another day in Orvieto.

# Goddesses di Cortona

There are eight of us and I think we are adding our ninth. The Goddesses di Cortona we have been dubbed. We pal together, sometimes all of us and most times we pair off in twos and threes, depending on our individual travel schedules. We are all independent, from all over the world and all walks of life.

Cortona is our thread embracing us and holding all of us together. Lay lines, we agree, is what brought us to Cortona, keeps us here and has brought all of us together. Never has Cortona seen such a pack of strong willed women with the determination to make Cortona home.

I have titled "our goddess" and Rut (now Isabella) is developing our website so our adventures can be read by all. We, as a group, are studying the lay lines to see how they may relate to us as individuals. We love Cortona!

Kandis is an artist from my part of the country, Highland Park. She came here to study art and to paint and show her art work three years ago, and like others fell in love and now lives here. I love her art shows; she is energetic and has so much pride in her translation through art of the Tuscany and Umbria areas. Kandis is young and single, I think in her early thirties, very close to her family but only returns home once a year. I have titled Kandis as the "Goddess of Art" I now have a lovely painting from her series of "Dancing Ladies," mine being The Worshiper, hanging in my living room.

Jennie, our traveler, lives for the moment and in the moment. I have titled her "Goddess of Travel." Jennie is single and (like me) in her 50's. She is English. She has traveled and stayed in Cortona for several years and has just bought a home in Cortona. She also has a home in Switzerland, in the Alps, as she is an avid skier as well as an artist. She finds great inspiration for her art in Cortona. My home now enjoys her art work.

Katerina, "Goddess Humanitarian" only barely describes this truly remarkable woman. Only in her thirties her accomplishments are way beyond a much older woman. She is an American having grown up in Canada. Katerina is a free spirit, an artist and a humanitarian. Katerina lived in Cortona for years; she felt she needed to move, so she bought a home in Lucca, a hilltop town between Florence and Pisa. She maintains an art gallery in Cortona and has several showings a year. But in my eyes, what makes her truly remarkable is her love for children, even though she has never been married and never wanted children for herself; she is a crusader of and for the orphans of Africa. She now lives many months each year at the convent and orphanage in Africa, teaching the children art.

Ruth, or Rut as the Italians who are not good with the the sound call her, has changed her name to Isabella and I have titled her "Goddess of Health." Ruth came to Cortona by accident, as a sailor, from England, she was hired on as crew to sail the Mediterranean. When the ship had troubles off the coast west of Siena, she jumped ship with a friend and stayed in a villa outside of Siena. The villa was occupied by sailors, all men and rough. Her friend offered her an apartment in Cortona to stay until the boat was repaired. It only took two days of her being in Cortona for her to fall in love and decide to stay. Besides being a sailor, Ruth is a healer. In her short month in Cortona she has developed more clients than most of the local physicians.

Amy our "Goddess of Foreign Marriage" is a 34-year-old, who lives in Camucia at the base of Cortona with her husband, Giovanni (yes, the tour guide who always gives me grief). Amy came to Cortona ten years ago as a student of Art History through the University of Georgia. Amy met Giovanni during her first week and for both of them it was love at first sight. She returned to New Orleans to complete her education but her heart was in Cortona with Giovanni. Although they both made many transatlantic trips to be together for short periods, they both realized they needed to be together and made the decision for Amy to move to Italy. They have just celebrated their tenth anniversary.

Donatella as her name now reads, changed from Donna, is another of our 50ish clan. She is from Seattle, Washington, and came to Cortona two years ago for a recovering vacation. Her husband of many years passed away and left Donatella devastated. After the funeral and a long grieving period, her friends convinced her to take a trip and find herself. She arrived in Cortona and was so overtaken by the town and the people she rented an apartment, left all of her things, returned to Seattle to settle the estate and came to Cortona, making Cortona her new home. I title her with great respect as the "Goddess of Happiness" which she has surely found in Cortona.

Then there is me, the "Goddess of Peace" as said by all of the Goddesses; it is I who walks into a room and complete peace surrounds all. That is what Cortona has given me, complete peace and a happiness I have never experienced. Cortona has become my inspiration for everything.

Vivienne is remarkably our true Goddess, our Goddess of Love, who loves all people wholeheartedly, taking from people only what they want to give and giving everything back. A truer friend we could never have as we have in Vivienne. She is married to Davide; he is a lucky man!

Finally, we are about to add Robin. I only just met Robin before I left Cortona to come home for a visit. I know her only well enough to have titled her "Goddess of Beauty" and to have enjoyed her art show in Cortona. She is a photographer and captures the true beauty of Tuscany. Her photos are the ones that you would, if you have not seen, swear the colors have been enhanced of the poppies, sunflowers and lilacs.

# My "Hell" in Pisa

It was a Wednesday morning and I found myself at the restaurant in the Pisa Airport absolutely detesting my trip to Pisa. Don't misunderstand me, Pisa can be and always has been, for me, an enchanting city, emitting history, art and, of course, the Duomo with Italy's most famous, "the leaning tower," the Baptistery, Camposanto, Museo due'Opera del Duomo and Museo dell' Sinopie.

My pre-planning of this trip to Pisa was flawless but soon fell apart. It was time to return home for a short visit with my family and friends. My return trip had been booked departing for Pisa. I thought to take full advantage of my travels in Italy, I would spend a couple of days in Pisa before catching the plane. I was looking forward to my first visit alone in Pisa.

The agenda would be mine, not someone else's. I could spend hours in the Duomo and even cry for the ruins caused by the bombings of 1944 to the Camposanto. There would be no one there to hurry me along as there had been in the past. I had arranged through the agency in Cortona, a week prior to travel, a room with a "bathtub," for two nights in a four star hotel (yes! a bathtub!) and I had purchased my train tickets and bus passes from Cortona to Florence and on to Pisa. Everything was perfect, a well planned excursion and I was going to have a bathtub, think bubble bath, for 2 entire days.

While packing, two days before I was to leave, I read my itinerary and to my horror, I realized my flight was booked a day earlier and now all of my travel accommodations were wrong and would have to be changed. I laughed at myself but thought, oh well! I returned to the agency to re-book, not really thinking it would be a big deal.

Three trips and five hours later at the agency I was told it was impossible to change my hotel reservations. The hotel said if I could not stay the two days, I would lose my reservation as they only booked two day stays. They would not even let me pay for two days and stay one night. The agency started checking other available hotels with vacancies and allowing accommodations for one night. They finally found me a room, but not only was I not going to have a bathtub, I was not even going to have a bathroom. The hotel had a single room for 45 euros but the bathroom was down the hall. After lots of translation by the agency to the hotel, they finally secured me a double room with a bath for 65 euros, but no bathtub for me. It should have dawned on me that a hotel for 65 euros with a bathroom in Pisa would have to be in the slums, but it did not. I was just thankful to have a room.

I have a wonderful new friend in Cortona, Angiolo, a man I met my second week in Cortona. Angiolo speaks no English and spends an hour or two a day teaching me Italian. I find the complete immersion into the language is a great way to learn.

When I voiced to Angiolo my disappointment in finding none of the restaurants in Cortona offered veal melanese on the menu, he told me to be patient and he would see what could be done. Only a day later he ask me to lunch; upon arriving at the restaurant he told me he had arranged, to my amazement, for me to have veal melanese. What a great surprise! He told me that the restaurants in Cortona being so close (around 28) and so many, did not fry foods that would give off strong odors in the city. Now I understand why there are no offensive odors of (I thought) fast foods or the smell of fried foods, having only fresh clean air with a hint of baking breads.

Having espresso and *dolci* the night before leaving, Angiolo told me he would come to my apartment at nine to collect my luggage and would drive me to the train station. What a great friend! I had been silently dreading dragging my luggage from my third floor apartment, down a steep hill, walking the three-fourths miles to the bus station and unloading from the bus, and loading to the train; now my trip was indeed getting better. Angiolo even loaded my bags onto the train!

I arrived in Florence finding the train to Pisa was running late, not a bad thing, it meant I had time for a cigarette and an espresso. Upon boarding the train to Pisa, trying to pull my big and very heavy suitcase onto the train, I pulled the ligaments in my right arm. From my elbow to my wrist my arm was useless and I was in great pain. The tips of my fingers tingled and I could not grip my hand. With hours of traveling ahead of me and luggage to tote, this was not a good thing. The train to Pisa takes over an hour, and not using my arm did make me feel better but I was very concerned as to how I was going to manage the rest of the trip.

When I arrived at the Pisa train station, I realized I would have to go down one set of stairs and up another set of stairs to get into the terminal. I found I could not even use my shoulder on my right side to carry either my purse or my laptop. Like an unbalanced pack mule, I loaded everything on my left shoulder and pulled my suitcase with my left hand slowly dragging it down one step at a time, walking the tunnel and pulling it up the other set of stairs, one by one, at a snail's pace. I kept thinking and praying it would not happen, that with all of the strain on my left side, I was surely going to pull my left arm or shoulder out. Much to my relief, other than pain and exhaustion, I made it to the terminal without dying. I exited the terminal, walked directly to the taxi stand and dropped everything. I gave the driver the name and address of the hotel and he said the hotel was less than a half mile and he would not go such a short distance. I explained to him my injuries, and feeling sorry for me, told me he would take me but would I pay 10 euros. What he did not realize was that I would have paid anything to be driven! He could have taken me to the cleaners. I gave him a great tip!

A wonderful elderly lady was at the front desk to check me in at the hotel. I gave her my name and told her I had a reservation for one night for a room with a bath and she gave me the key and told me my room was on the third floor.

I asked for the location of the elevator. She told me they didn't have an elevator, I would have to take the stairs. Well, I need a bellboy, but no bellboy! Tears, pain and frustration! By some miracle I made it to my room, took two pain pills (from my *mal di denti*) and fell onto the bed. I awoke hours later, in less pain, hungry and knowing I was not going to be site-seeing in Pisa. I thought I better go eat and just come back to bed. My arm was so bad I could not even carry my purse.

I put money, my passport and the room key in my pocket and left the hotel (my hotel had no dining) to find a nearby restaurant. I walked for blocks and blocks, making right turns, left turns and though alleys looking for anyplace to eat. I realized I was in China town (in Pisa) and it seemed nothing like Italy, not one Italian restaurant.

I finally saw a sign *"il bar"*! It didn't look like much more than a hole in the wall, so I thought I would grab a fast sandwich and return to the hotel. I was seated, handed a menu, a napkin was placed in my lap and a bread basket arrive in fluid motion and all at one time. The menu was extensive, the place was spotless and the waiters very friendly. I decided to try the food and ordered a full meal. It was absolutely one of the finest meals I had in all of Italy. I had melon with *prosciutto*, baked chicken, seasoned vegetables with olive oil, and fried polenta and *panna cotta* for dessert. *Vino della casa* was excellent and I topped it all off with espresso and the waiter (free) brought out cheese and fruit. How delightful! I was full, not feeling much pain and back to being happy.

When I left the restaurant it was getting dark and being in the slums of Pisa, I was feeling somewhat afraid. That's when it dawned on me, I did not know where my hotel was, not only did I not know where it was, I didn't remember the name. My goodness, what a terrible feeling. I had left my purse with the name and address in the hotel.

I walked through the slums, back alleys and over railroad tracks, with barking dogs, homeless people and driven by fear for three hours before I finally found my hotel. I honestly wanted to fall to my knees and thank God when I looked down the street and saw the neon, flashing sign of my hotel.

I must plan a new trip to Pisa, with all the enjoyment of the true Pisa, very soon, as I do not want this experience to linger in my mind!

# London, England

Scones and Devonshire Cream! Could life be better? I have never been a great lover of English cuisine so when I visit I tend to live off Bangers and Mash, Fish and Chips and warm scones with Devonshire cream. Yes, I always gain weight while in London. I have scones (not a scone) for breakfast and at tea time, and always with Devonshire cream. To make it worse, I am never happy with one pot of the cream, always requesting a second pot.

I have searched all over Dallas for Devonshire cream. Finally, since not even Central Market carries it, and they carry everything, I have decided Devonshire cream is London's best kept secret and they do not export.

I had been home for a short visit and when making my return reservations, I was told there would be a seven hour layover at London's Gatwick Airport. There is nothing like sitting in an airport for seven hours after a nine and a half hour flight. I weighed the situation and decided just to stay and spend a couple of days in London. Gatwick Airport is very large and you have to walk, I'm sure, three miles to reach your luggage, or in my case, the smoking lounge. Having flown from Dallas I really wanted a cigarette and this long walk was not making me happy.

They have conveyor belts for the luggage but the people have to walk; it just doesn't seem fair. But it could have been worse. I did fly business class, I did get off the airplane with the first wave of people and there were carts still available, so I did not have to carry my carry-on bags.

Arriving in London very early in the morning, I arrived at my hotel just in time for those to-die-for warm scones and potted cream. How delightful. I had the front desk hold my luggage and had scones before I even checked in. What a perfect start to my visit in London. Having thoroughly enjoyed my breakfast, I continued to check in and get my luggage to my room so I could visit London. I took a complete departure from my past visits to London. Instead of staying in the city, I stayed at a Country Inn about five miles outside the city.

My inn had three restaurants, a wonderful English bar and beautiful gardens with a stream. Lazing around the stream are ducks and the largest swans waiting to be hand fed. I hired a driver from the hotel to take me into London with designated times and places to pick me up. My first afternoon was spent walking the city and window shopping. I think this is the only trip in my life that I actually did not shop, other than buying a tour book. Like all large cities, it is impossible to see everything you want to see. London is a city with many interests, and my interests being far and wide, I found myself scattered over miles and miles of this beautiful and intriguing city.

It also caused me to miss and appreciate Cortona. I just about know every nook and cranny in Cortona and I know where to find everything. Not so in London; however, without the difficulties of a different language and having a driver familiar with the city, things went very smoothly and I got to see much more than if I had been on my own. Hiring a driver is less expensive than renting a car or using a taxi service and you never have to wait for parking.

I told my driver to drop me at Harrods for two hours and gave him a list of all the places I wanted to see in London. He told me to go shop and he would map out the best routes and have it ready by the time I finished at Harrods. And we think we need husbands . . . not!

I love Harrods and I love the fact that a foreigner can own a place like Harrods in London. Harrods at Knightsbridge is a great place to shop or to just spend a couple of hours looking at everything and eating scones in the restaurant. I have shopped all of my life, often thinking I was truly addicted to shopping. What I have come to understand is that I am not addicted to shopping, I simply shop out of boredom. I am never bored in Europe and really don't feel the need to shop. It also helps that my casa in Cortona is small, furnished and I don't like carrying any more than I have to. I have learned my lesson.

Surprising even myself, I returned to my driver without shopping bags. He said I was the only woman he had ever taken to Harrods that did not return loaded with shopping bags. I told him, I was indeed a different type of woman.

I went for a walk in Regent's Park with the roses still in bloom and the temperature perfect. I wonder how many people go to London and just take strolls in the parks. It is a lovely thing to do and the people are great and love to tell you about the city. After Regent's Park, I wanted to go somewhere I had never been. My driver, Anton, suggested Little Venice. Brightly painted, long narrow boats line the Regent's Canal between the affluent Maida Avenue and Bloomfield Road. These boats are covered with splendid blooms in hanging baskets. Three canals converge and there is a floating café where I had Banger's and Mash and iced tea. We all know tea is the drink of England but that is "hot tea"; it appeared to be an ordeal when I ordered iced tea. The tea arrived about the time I finished my Banger's and Mash.

My last treat for the day was a visit to the Somerset House which contains three galleries. The Courtauld Institute of Art Gallery has Impressionist and Post-Impressionist paintings, Gauguin's "Nevermore," Monet's "Bar at the Folies-Bergere" and Van Gogh's "Self Portrait with Bandaged Ear." The Hermitage Rooms echo the style of the famous namesake museum in St Petersburg and have changing displays on loan from the Hermitage collection. The Gilbert Collection focuses on the decorative arts, with a glittering array of gilt snuff boxes, European silverware and jewel-encrusted objet d'art. I ate, yes again, at the French restaurant The Admiralty's Summer Café on the River Terrace. The terrace runs the length of the building on the Thames side which you can stroll along while waiting on your meal. I could just see St Paul's and the Gothic towers of Westminster. We arrived back at the hotel, just in time to see a garden wedding. Not wanting to interrupt the ceremony, we just sat in the car and watched. I don't think there is a more beautiful wedding than one held in a garden full of glorious flowers.

The next day I went on a driving tour of London and then of the surrounding areas. The first part of the tour was a blur; we took the autobahns so we could start at Westminster, stopping at the Buckingham Palace Gardens and on to Chelsea and back to Knightsbridge. In Kensington we stopped at Holland Park, walked around the Holland House and had tea and scones. From there we went to the Tower of London, on River Thames, then we were off to Soho and Covent Garden. We drove the Mall Strand at St James's Park and Piccadilly to Knightsbridge entering Hyde Park. We stopped at a deli and bought a picnic basket for lunch and ate in the park. This was my best day ever in London.

When we returned to the hotel I was almost sad that I had not booked a longer stay, but I felt I had enjoyed the very best of London. I checked out the night before I left as I had to get the bus at 6 am the next morning. I told the concierge I was hating that I would be leaving before the scones for breakfast would be ready. Guess what, the next morning at 5:30 he had two, fresh out of the oven warm scones and potted cream delivered to my room. Yes, I will always stay at Country Inns when visiting London.

# Io Ritorno a Cortona

I was excited about returning to Cortona from London, even if I did have to wake up at 5:00 am; of course the scones being delivered improved my mood greatly. I caught a 7:45am flight from Gatwick to Pisa.

I love these European airlines, first Air France and now British Air. The seats are leather, large and comfortable but it is the meals they serve that take my breath away. For breakfast on this trip, they served me scrambled eggs, sausage, ham, fruit and warm scones with coffee and juice. Yes, I had already had scones but I did not turn these away.

When I arrived in Pisa, I did not even look at the city. I collected my bag and went directly to buy my train ticket, walked the length of the airport (very small), out of the north exit and got right on the train to *Firenze*. When I arrived in *Firenze*, I had to wait an hour for the train to Camucia, just enough time to smoke and have a real, Italian espresso.

Watching the ever changing train schedule, the bin numbers do not appear until about 10 minutes before boarding. The bin number for Camucia came up as number 14. I boarded the train, arranged my luggage, storing the large suitcase up top and got comfortable for the last leg of my trip.

I am home, and the Italian way is for everything to change at the last minute, which it did. At three minutes before departure a man boarded the train and said, "If anyone is going to Rome (the train to Camucia) they just changed the bin number, the train is now leaving out of bin 8." Holy goodness, there is no way I can run with all of my stuff and board another train in three minutes.

The other thing I love about Italy, the gentlemen are fabulous. A man sitting across the aisle, seeing my distress, grabbed my bag from overhead and said, "Stay close." We ran to the train, he re-arranged my bags, gave me a bottle of water and said, *"Una bella giornata."* I love Italy!

Amy called me on my cell phone to see what time I would be arriving in Camucia and to let me know she would be waiting at the station to take me to Cortona. This has been a great trip!

Amy drove all the way up my hill to drop me and my bags off. She returned to park the car and I told her I would meet her in Piazza. Entering the piazza, I felt like I had just arrived back home. The first person I saw was Angiolo and after hugs and kisses, the three of us went for coffee at Piazza Signorelli.

People started coming to the table, welcoming me back to Cortona. Kandis had been painting all day, and was, in fact, covered in paint. She had a great art opening in July and her next opening is the first week in October.

We saw Jennie; she has finished her watercolors and has an art opening at La Galleria Gino Severini, September 10–16. This will be her first solo showing and she is very nervous. I told her not to worry, all of us Goddesses would be there to support her.

I had dinner with Peter and Jeffery the second night. They had moved from their country villa to a casa in Cortona. We walked over for me to see the house. It is a stand alone house (very rare in Cortona) with a two car garage. The house is just above the partaire looking over the entire Cortonese valley.

Rocco and Rapiphan have returned to Thailand so Rapi can have the baby at home. Rut has found an apartment and moved. Her healing business is going fairly well and surprisingly gossip has it she is dating a new doctor that has moved to town. I'll have to find out if this is true! A doctor and a healer!

Katerina e-mailed Amy; she will be in Cortona on September 15 for a couple of weeks and asked me to arrange for all of the goddesses to get together for dinners.

Everything is the same at the beauty shop; Nuccio and Sabrina were glad to have me back and told me all of the new gossip in town.

Angiolo got tickets for me and Amy to go to the *Mostra Mercato Nazionale dell'Antiquariato* and a new museum is opening on Sunday.

My third day back home was Donatella's birthday. Several of us, Amy, Ruth, Kandis and I had dinner together. Donatella said it was her favorite birthday.

I went to the *Immobiliaria* to pay my rent and Roberto gave me my first utility bill. In Cortona, they bill you every three months and it appears, if I am reading this correctly, it is a bill for gas, water and electric. I guess not having central air conditioning has its rewards. My total bill is 55.94 euros. Where in America can you get utilities for $55 for three months? I think I might be very surprised in *inverno (*winter*)*, they say the gas can cost $400 a month for an apartment my size. Peter said last year he paid 7,000 euros for gas for a three month period. We shall see.

Everyone is shocked that I will be staying here for Christmas. It will make me a real Cortonese. Peter has a great house and we have already decided that is where we will put our Chrismas tree. Several of us are staying for Christmas: Kandis, Peter, Jeffery, Ruth, Donatella and me. I think it will be a wonderful Christmas. We will all cook and drink during the holidays at Peter's. Jennie wants us to all come for a visit at her casa in the Swiss Alps during January and of course there is the carnival in Venice in February to which we will all go.

Mara, *mia amica* that owns the Brazilian restaurant, wants me to spend part of the winter with her in Brazil. I would love to go to Brazil but it is important to me to go to Africa to help in the orphanage. I don't know how I will fit everything into a good schedule. I'll play Scarlet and think about it tomorrow.

Things have changed but it is pretty much like I left it and I am glad to be home!

# Tuscany

I have discovered the perfect, the ultimate way to travel in and learn about Tuscany. Find the perfect travel mate who has always lived in the area, who loves Tuscany and who loves to talk about Tuscany.

I have found my perfect travel mate; it is Angiolo. Angiolo is 58, has lived in a palace in Cortona all of his life and until two months ago (he retired) worked in *Firenze*. Angiolo speaks no English (other than, Stop! Wait one moment.) and has the patience of a god while teaching me Italian.

Before I returned to Dallas for a visit, Angiolo and I had become great friends and I could tell he was hoping for more. We would date several times a week, visiting churches, museums and walking the fields of poppies and sunflowers. He brought desserts to my house and helped entertain Terrell when she came to town. We had coffee dates, dinner dates and prosecco dates. He helped me with my Italian and we just had great fun together.

When I returned to Cortona, Angiolo was the first person I saw in the piazza and other than nights, we have been together *sempre* (always). He has dedicated himself as my personal tour guide and wants to teach me about every hilltop town in Tuscany and in Umbria.

Our first visit was to Pienza known for their pecorino cheese. I had indulged (in Cortona) in ricotta cheese with honey but I found the divine pecorino cheese in Pienza served with honey or with fig marmalade . . . oh my gosh. I just want to eat cheese.

We went in a local cheese shoppe, after a wonderful lunch of *formaggio* con honey and vino, so I could get percorino cheese for mia casa. For lunch I had ordered *formaggio* mista which is an assortment of four pecorino cheeses with honey. I was naïve in thinking there were only four types of pecorino cheese. The shoppe was filled with so many different types of Pecorino cheese, I felt lost. I wanted a sample package to take home, made easy for a lame shopper. I expressed my dismay to Angiolo, he said, "Stop! Wait one moment."

He and the shoppe owner spoke *rapido italiano* for several minutes and the shoppe owner announced to me there was not a problem. He began cutting small slices of cheese from all over the store, saying things like, "This is great, you can't do without; try this, oh and this is a must." I now have a box of cheese that may last my entire stay in Cortona. I also have different types of honey, figs and other marmalades.

I cannot describe all the different pecorino cheese other than you can get it soft, young and sweet, or aged and hard. The more aged, the less sweet and the riper the aroma. There are also many ways to age the pecorino, one way is in ashes but anyway you have it, you will delight in the many different flavors and textures. Next time you have a wine party be sure and add the honey and fig; you will be a hit!

Pienza is a small town but very rich in history; a town you will not want to miss on a visit to Tuscany. Pienza is located in the land of Siena in the Orcia Valley, just uphill from Montepulciano. Not being near the rail system, many overlook Pienza; such a shame. It is of Renaissance architecture and the birthplace of Pope Pio II, full of hidden surprises and breathtaking vistas. Recent archeological findings testify that the origins of the population of this area is very old, already in IV-V millennium BC up to the settlement of the Etruscans and the Romans. Pope Pio II constructed (1459–62) a group of monumental buildings: Piccolomini Palace (at the place where he was born), the Cathedral, the town hall and the Palace of the Cardinal Borgio (The Bishop's Palace).

The square dedicated to Pope Pio II is the landmark of Pienza and is the heart of the longitudinal axis of the road, Corso Rosselino, which connects the two principal entrances of the city: "Porta al Ciglio" and "Porta al Murello." If you visit this beautiful city, do not miss the "Museum of the Cathedral" and remember the Tuscany area was the home of the many of the most famous artists.

We made our way from Pienza, across the Val d'Orcia on to Montepulciano. I had, not long after I moved to Cortona, visited Montepulciano for it's well known wine festival.

On my first visit, the streets were crowded with tourist and locals, packed to the point I could barely see anything but the costumes and wine displays. This visit was completely different and very enjoyable, especially since I was with quite the "art historian" and tour guide.

Unlike Pienza, Montepulciano is a large hilltop town with a towering castle and high stone walls and many Palaces.

# Tuscany by Car

I have owned and driven cars for almost forty years. I've been in traffic jams, accidents and I have gotten my share of speeding tickets. We all take cars for granted, always having one and it being our main mode of transportation. We rarely think of the expense of cars: gas, insurance and the car payments. Without thinking we just hop in our cars and go!

Without a thought of my dependency on a car, I moved to a country where I cannot even, as a non-citizen, buy a car, and to a community if I could buy a car, could not even house a car. Without owning a car, I am completely dependent on trains, buses, walking or occasionally hitching a ride with a friend, sometimes with people I don't even know.

It's amazing that I do not miss driving. I don't miss traffic, or pumping my own gas or getting a car inspected; I just don't miss any of the "things" that go with owning a car. I do love the trains and autobuses of Europe. Italians make, for the most part, travel very convenient and not very costly.

I have, notwithstanding some oops, learned the train and bus schedules and how best to avoid the strikes, and how to adjust for late arrival times. Most of the places I want to visit in Italy are on the rail lines or bus routes. I spent days making maps and lists of all of the sites I wanted to see during my year in Cortona.

Some of my designated "must see" spots, while being possible to get to without a car, take great planning. The hilltop towns take the most planning to make sure that from the rail station there will be available transportation to the hilltop. The stations are at the bottom. Some (very few) have taxis to deliver you to the top, others have buses and in the case of Orvieto, you must take the funicular, then there are others where you must walk. Sometimes (most times) the walks are an event in themselves and you must be in pretty great shape or you just skip that town, call it a mistake and get back on the train. I am guilty!

Luckily, with some exceptions (laughable), I have managed to travel through Italy with ease and pleasure on the trains and buses and I always enjoyed the few taxi trips and the drivers are a hoot! But one of the best parts of my stay has been the great friends I have made and their desire for my year to be memorable, fun and educational.

I have Peter and Jeffery, always asking me to go places with them, in their car. They have taken me to wonderful country restaurants, cooking schools in the Tuscan hills, to feast on grand dinners prepared by the students of the school, while enjoying the best of country inns and spectacular vistas. I have gone on out of town trips with them to the Dolomites, the Lagos of Italy, Verona, Castiglion Fiorentino to the beefsteak festival and simple drives in the hills of Tuscany. We have made special day visits to Florence, Milano and Bologna.

Angiolo has made it his life's ambition for me to see and learn all about every hilltop town in Tuscany and Umbria. He has a weekly planning schedule of where we are going and always plans the most scenic routes, avoiding the convenience of the autobahns. In a short time, we have covered Siena's Chianti region, Pienza, Montepulciano, Lucignano, Gaiole, Perugia and Assisi. A couple of nights per week, we always drive to Lago Trasimeno for drinks.

With Amy, I am always going to Siena. She drove us to Siena on my first visit to Cortona, and every time someone comes for a visit, whether visiting her or me, they always want to see Siena, so off we go in Amy's car. I am sure Amy is sick of Siena but she is a great sport about going. During my many trips to Castiglion del Lago ( seven trips to the dentist), she drove me twice, always stopping in Terontola for cappuccino.

Gino or Giuliano are always in Piazza Garibaldi where the bus stop is, available and always offering me a ride to the train station or to Camucia. Gino and I have finally become friends. He stopped talking to me for months when I told him there would be no *"romantico o d' amore."* He's gotten over that and is very nice now.

*Allora, Giuliano* is a totally different story. Since my first week in Cortona, this man has followed me everywhere. He lives near me and is always lurking around my building, waiting for me to come or go. Anywhere I am dining, I can be sure to look up and find him standing in the street just staring at me. He has sent his daughter, *chiama* Sara, to tell me he loves me. Massimo has had to run him off several times from me at the Fusion Bar. Then, just before I left town, he started sending flowers to *mia casa*. Yikes!

The night before I left for America, Angiolo and Amy stopped by my house for a visit. When Angiolo saw the flowers, he asked all kinds of questions: who are they from, why is he sending them. I think there is a little jealously going on. I saw Giuliano in the piazza today. I was waiting for the bus to go to Arezzo. He had bought a new car saying he thought I might date him if he had a nice car. Oh no! He also told me that while I was in America, Angiolo had told him that I was his girlfriend and to leave me alone. I had to agree to make Giuliano back off, but Angiolo's girlfriend? I think I now have a new problem. I also have a wonderful friend that owns the Brazilian restaurant in Cortona, *si chiama Mara*. She lives here from April until the last of October and then returns to Brazil to run her other restaurant there. She is the true Brazilian with that beautiful Brazilian "butt" that Americans fly to Brazil to get. She is always taking me to her club to sunbathe, swim and exercise; see, I really don't need a car!

My friends have been very kind to include me in car trips to all of the festival events. We have been to towns celebrating: wines, cheese, truffles, beef, flowers and so many of the great sporting events. I find myself being the luckiest person in the world. All of these wonderful experiences have been made possible by great new friends that will be friends forever.

I can live in Italy and in Cortona without having to ever worry about all of the nuances of owning a car.

# Arezzo

Arezzo is one of the wealthiest cities in Tuscany, producing gold jewelry for shops all over Europe. It is famous for Piero della Francesca's frescoes in San Francesco. Arezzo is a town very near me, one I have been through many times but had not spent time visiting.

I especially wanted to visit this the first weekend in September to take advantage of the monthly market and this was the weekend of Joust of the Saracen.

The Joust of Saracen (Giostra del Saracino) is held each year in the Piazza Grande. The tournament dates back to the Crusades in the Middle Ages, when all Christendom dedicated itself to driving the North African Arabs (the Moors) out of Europe.

There are lively and colorful processions preceding the event, in which eight costumed knights charge toward a wooden effigy of the Saracen. The aim is to try to hit the Saracen's shield with lances and then avoid a cat-o'-three-tails swinging back and unseating them from their horses. Each pair of knights represents one of Arezzo's four rival contrade (districts) and their supporters occupy a side each of Piazza Grande. They are quiet when their own contrada knights are jousting, but make as much noise as possible to distract the opposition. The winner receives a gold lance.

Amy's husband (Giovanni) had tours all day Sunday, so Amy and I decided to make a day in Arezzo. I had dinner with Peter Saturday and Amy called late (11:00) to let me know there was a bus from Cortona to Camucia at 9:55 and that if I could catch that bus she would meet me at the train station for a 10:20 train to Arezzo. I told Amy that was great, "A pui tardi, ciao, ciao!" It is only a 5 minute bus ride and a 20 minute train ride to Arezzo and with the bus and train schedules complimenting each other, one can be and should be in Arezzo within 30 minutes. Not in my life!

Waking Sunday morning was tough; I had been out until two having dinner with Peter, and drinking with friends at the Fusion Bar. I am too old for such! But, I did get up in time and was looking forward to my day in Arezzo. In one of my short stops in Arezzo, I had found a lacquered serving tray that was hand painted with a scene of Cortona that I wanted to get Quay for her birthday.

I got up, got dressed and headed into to town to buy my bus and train tickets and have a cappuccino and a *pasta con crema* before catching the bus to Camucia. I arrived at the bus stop in Piazza Garibaldi forty minutes early. I love being early; I always carry my Italian study guide and take the time to study. I settled in to wait for the bus and to study my *Italiano*. At 9:55 am, I put away my book getting ready for the bus. At 10:00 the bus had still not arrived; I waited a few minutes before calling Amy to tell her I was apparently going to be late.

When I called Amy, she said, "That's the Italian bus' for you."

At 10:05, I walked over to the posted bus schedule to make sure Amy had gotten the time correct. I was trying to read the schedule when the little crazy man (thinks he works for the bus company) came over saying, *"Posso? Oggi es Domenica.* No bus service until 1:30 pm."

I called Amy and she sent Giovanni to bring me down to Camucia saying we still had time to catch the 10:20 to Arezzo. Giovanni got me to the station at 10:17, just in time.

We stamped our tickets and ran to track one, a little breathless but in time for the train. We waited about 20 minutes for the train thinking it was just late and finally we checked the train schedule. Guess what? It's Sunday and that train doesn't run on Sunday. We both laughed and just waited for the 11:30 train, the one that actually runs on Sunday.

Finally*, noi arriviamo ad Arezzo.* This is a great town but you do a lot of walking and up some steep hills, but hey! Hills, I'm used to it; I live in Cortona, the city of steep hills!

The town was full of activity; the brilliant costumes of the parade and the men on horseback were so much fun to see and to watch parading around. They stop the procession often, waiting for flag throwers and such. During one of their stops, Amy, being the photographer, thought it would be a great picture of me standing behind the horses. I told Amy it was fairly dangerous to stand behind a horse but she convinced me it would only take a moment. Ha, in that moment I was backed into and almost run over by a horse. A great moment!

We first went to Piazza Grande; it is a square famous for its regular antiques markets but today it was set up for the "Joust" and full of activity. The façade of the Palazzo della Fraternita dei Laici is decorated with a relief of the Virgin (1434) by Bernardo Rossellino. The lower half of the building dates from 1377. The belfry and clock tower are from 1552. The north side of the square is occupied by a beautiful arcade designed by Vasari in 1573. I am still amazed by the age and architecture of these wonderful buildings.

The things you must visit in Arezzo: Pieve di Santa Maria, which you get to by following the main shopping street, Corso Italia, the Fortezza Medicea e Parco built for Cosimo I during the 16$^{th}$ c, excellent views across the Arno valley and also from Parco il Prato, a public park. Take a picnic basket, eat and just watch the people. Some of the other incredible buildings are the Duomo, Museo del Duomo, Museo Statale d'Arte Medioevale e Moderna and the Anfiteatro Romano e Museo Archeologico.

Casa del Vasari is worth a visit; you may have to ring the doorbell if it is not open. Vasari built this house for himself in 1540 and decorated the ceilings and walls with portraits of fellow artists, friends and mentors. He also painted himself looking out of one of the windows.

Santa Maria delle Grazie, completed in 1449 and set in its own walled garden, is a church on the south-eastern outskirts of the town.

You might want to book a room at Castello di Gargonza, more of a "medieval castle-cum-village" with just 25 rooms. A sweeping tree-lined driveway curves around the castle walls to the entrance. There is a tiny garden and a pretty frescoed chapel where services are held once a week.

Of course, you must visit the famous San Francesco, the 13c Church of San Francesco contains Piero della Francesca's frescoes, the Legend of the True Cross, his masterpiece and one of Italy's greatest fresco cycles.

I have to go back next month for the market, which is held the first weekend of each month. Today, with all of the landmarks of the city, we only had time for fast walks through the market. There are hand-made crafts from all over Tuscany.

It had turned out, even with the mix-up on the bus and the train, one of my favorite days. It was now time to take the walk back to the train station and go home. The end of a beautiful day. Well, not quite the end. We arrived at the train station five minutes before it was due to depart and boarded the train. We got into deep and funny conversations not at all keeping track of the time. I, at one time, looked at my watch, wondering what time we would arrive in Camucia as it was only a 20 minute ride.

After something like close to an hour, Amy looked at me with eyes the size of saucer's her hand over her month and said, "Oh holy cow! We are on the wrong train, we are on the train to Firenze!"

Right! Firenze is going the wrong direction, we needed to be going towards Roma.

It was still a beautiful day and one that I will not forget! Thanks Amy!

# *Vorrei Comprare una Casa a Cortona*
(have I lost my mind?)

After only a few months in Cortona, I decided that I wanted to sell my house in Frisco and buy a smaller one in Dallas and also have a home *qui a* Cortona. Nice thought. Wrong! I met with Roberto, my *Immobiliario*, and asked his advice on homes, flats, or condos in Cortona. We made arrangements to visit a lovely two story home in the heart of Cortona.

I was very excited about seeing it because of its location and it has *"il giardino."* Roberto did not know the price; he handles the weekly rentals but knew the owner would sell. He said he would find the price before we visited tomorrow.

I was *molto* excited about the property and the fact that all of the properties come furnished. I knew where the property was located and even though I could not get in, I had to walk by just to look at the outside. It is considered a single family residence even though it is attached on either side.

It was easy to find and upon arriving I was even more intrigued. There is a high, maybe 8 foot rock wall with a rounded wooden door and a heavy lock. It appeared to be a door into the garden. I could not see over the stone wall but I knew enough to get me excited. In fact I was awake most of the night just thinking about what it may look like. I met Angiolo for cappuccino at 9:00 the next morning and told him about the property.

He offered to go with me at 10:00 to view the property. I was almost skipping to Roberto's office.

We were way early but Roberto had the key and said the time was no problem. *Andiamo!* We were off to see, possibly, my new home. I will really be able to say "I live in Cortona."

Now before I spoke to Roberto about buying a house, I had spoken to every home owner I knew to find out all of the ins and out of buying a home. I spoke to homeowners who have lived here all of their lives. I spoke to foreigners who have purchased a home here.

I heard horror stories about the price changing, the *immobiliario* or the attorney wanting more money at the last minute. I heard about how to pay money under the table so the taxing authorities would not know the true price.

It seemed I must prepare myself for verbal fighting with loud voices, the threats of law suits; the list of horrors just went on and on. However, most people did close on the houses and were happy afterwards. It must be very exciting for an Italian to sell a home and get to go through all of the ado. I was not real sure I wanted to get involved in all of the fuss but it seemed if I truly wanted a home in Cortona, I would have no choice.

All of the information I had learned failed to dissuade me and I continued with the idea of owning a home in Cortona.

As soon as I saw Roberto, I asked if he had spoken to the owner. He assured me that he had and that the owner would sell. When I asked him, *"Quanto costa?"*

He said, "Let's look at it first and then we can discuss the price."

Sure enough that wonderful wood door was the passage to the garden. It is a small garden with a patio and a bird bath and roses covering almost the entire garden . . . lovely. It's a good start to my falling in love. There is a covered terrace with two steps up to the front door and there is a balcony upstairs. Yes, yes, I am falling in love!

When you enter the house, you enter into one room serving (like my apartment) as the kitchen, dining and living room. It was small but I really wasn't looking for anything very large. It has a well appointed kitchen, by that I mean it has a dishwasher unlike my current apartment.

At the end of the room is a spiral staircase to the upstairs. I asked Roberto how they furnished the upstairs. He said they brought the furniture over the upstairs balcony and through the window. Okay then, this would stop me from replacing any furniture; sounds like a money saver to me!

At the top of the staircase is a large landing which was furnished with a twin bed, a chair and a telephone table. Not that there was a telephone. Again this is a 650-year-old house but does not necessarily mean it has ever been wired for a telephone. I had to ask Roberto and thank you, he informed me it had been wired.

The one and only bathroom is upstairs; this still does not deter me. I am looking on the bright side and just thinking an upstairs bathroom means more exercise for me, a good thing. Oh, there is no bathtub, again that is okay, I am now accustomed to showers. I'm still falling in love here.

The bedroom is very nice and furnished beautifully and even actually has a closet. Okay, it's looking good. When I stepped out on the balcony I could see the panoramic view of the valley over the rooftops of the city. Very nice! Yes, I think, I am in love! Oh no, oh no! There is no dryer, but to make it worse there is no washing machine; even worse, the house has not been wired for a washing machine. I am deeply saddened, but I find a small door opening to the attic; there is a small space behind this door and it is next to the bathroom. I asked Roberto if it was possible to knock through the wall getting to the water and putting the washer there. He said it did not look like a problem and it was tall enough behind the door to get the combo washer and dryer.

Okay, I am set and I want this house. Now true, the house is very tiny having only 90m but I do live alone and it does have an extra bed and a garden and terrace and balcony. Yes, I want to buy it and I tell Roberto!

We returned to Roberto's office to discuss the price. Are you ready for this? The price is 272,000 euros which depending on the exchange rate is 330,000 to 350,000 US Dollars. Holy cow, am I buying Cortona!

Besides the price there is the cost of the *immobiliario* the attorney, the plumber, the electrician, the banker, and whatever other brother is under the table. All of this for 800 sq. ft. I was so depressed, I will never own a home in Cortona.

My current apartment is 590 euros a month and I figure if I live here for six months every year, at what it would cost me to buy the house, I could live in my apartment for 72 years and that would include the cost of the utilities and the upkeep. Oh my, I am not owning a home in Cortona, not at the cost of over 450 dollars a square foot! I think I am no longer in love.

# Lucignano

It's late; I am very tired having been gone all day and walking most of the day. I visited the best town in all of Tuscany today, did not take notes and want to write about it before I lose even one memory of this very special town.

Before I moved to Cortona, while still in Dallas, I studied Tuscany and chose "must see" cities. The city or Citta di Lucignano was my favorite study. Because of its circular street plan, Tucany's best-preserved medieval architecture and its defensive towers, it was a city first on my list to visit.

Lucignano is not on a rail line or a bus route, making it a difficult place for me to visit without a car or someone willing to take me there. I hinted to several people but didn't have any offers to take me. Actually most of the Italians said, "ah its small, not much there . . . yada yada yada!" I didn't think I was going to ever get there.

My friend Angiolo, being most willing to take me anywhere, chose today, as a surprise to me, to visit Lucignano. Yesterday, he said be ready for a trip tomorrow at 9:00, not telling me where we were going. Lucignano is only about 40k's from here so it wasn't long until I guessed where we were headed.

I know every time I write about something in Italy, I always say things like, this is the best or prettiest or greatest trip I have ever been on but I have been wrong. Nothing compares to Lucignano. It is indescribable.

First it is the design of the *città,* the street plan is extremely unusual, consisting of a series of four concentric rings encircling the hill upon which the town sits, sheltered by its ancient walls. There are four small piazzas at the center. The *Collegiata* is fronted by some attractive steps whose circular shape reflects the town's street plan. I liken it to my grandmother's chocolate meringue pie with its high peek in the center being like the *Collegiata* and circular steps leading to circular streets.

When I read about Lucignano, I was so intrigued by the architecture, wondering how the buildings would fit into the circular plans of the *strade*. The buildings are mostly connected with stores on the bottom and residencies above for two, three or four floors. Well, the buildings curve fitting right into the curvatures of the *strade*. It's too beautiful to even imagine. And all of this was built in the 13 and 14c's.

It was market day in Lucignano and all of the people were out and about even though there was a very slight rain. I started looking at the people and thinking, oh my, in all my photography I have truly forgotten something that is perhaps the most important of my living here in Italy. The people, I have not been photographing the people of Italy.

I went crazy with this idea. I started going up to people saying, "*Posso, mi photograph tu, or lei o lui?*" True, the Italians being somewhat shy and private, some thinking me crazy, others very flattered, some posing, and some blushing with embarrassment. But I have now started probably my most prized photo album.

I know I am especially going to love the shots of the elderly, laughing at me with their near toothless smiles and the babies, with their inquiring looks. Oh what fun!

The character of the faces of the aging Italians is priceless. We had lunch at the most divine place, *Ristorante La Rocca*, in city centre. *Cucina tipica delle Toscana con piatti locali e Tartufo.*

Now when I have shared eating experiences with you, I usually say, I ate, I dined, I pigged out; today, I feasted! I started out with *Fantasia di Crostini, un misto of crostini con funghi, con patè, con spinaci, e con pomodoro. Secondo* I had *Fagottini alla Rocca*, this is a pasta with cream, ham and spinach, yum; then *Anatra in Porchetta*, a roast suckling duck *con Verdure Grigliate* all accompanied with *Campo Del Monte (1999) vino.* NO . . . *dolci per me!* Please, wheel my fat body out of here!

With all of that, I have not even touched the best part of my day. After this wonderful lunch, I had to walk (just wanted to nap). We had covered the city and because the city sits way up on the top of a high hill, I wanted to walk outside of the walls and take pictures of the valley below. The valley is beautiful with hues of all shades, large cypress trees, vinyards for miles, olive trees and still blooming flowers.

Once you leave the walls of Lucignano, the outer portion is one flowing garden after another with a coffee bar here and there. The gardens are so lush and it's difficult to tell where one ends and another begins. We stopped to take a coffee and I noticed a large arched rock arbor leading into another garden, the opening large enough for a car, with heavy iron gates that were standing open. I was curious so we went to take a look. Upon entering this garden a man stopped and told us it was his property but please feel free to stroll and look. I was delighted, this was truly a "garden of Eden" with a casa so grand, I have never seen a casa so large. I asked him if it was all one residence.

This delightful man, *nome Luigi Moriani*, loved that I was so enchanted with his place that he started telling me everything about it, and that it had been in his family for generations, since 1532. I asked him if it was a castle, a casa or a villa, and how he would describe it?

He said, "*Non, non è un castle, non è una casa, non è una villa, it is a museo storico.*"

"*Why a museo storico?*"

"There are no words, I must take you a tour and your eyes will tell you everything you want to know."

I spent hours with this man, and he told me I could come anytime, stay for free and photograph or write about his place, the town and the surrounding villas. He treated me like I was long lost family.

He is neither a young man nor an old man. He is slightly crippled on one side, some side teeth missing, very animated and very proud. I liked him immediately, and I loved all of the stories he shared with me. He is very excited when he talks in his native tongue with enough English thrown in for me to understand and he laughs at himself and his stories.

The "*museo storico's*" main building stands four stories with also an attic, made of stones with shuttered windows, cupola, and more chimneys than I could count. There may be thirty fireplaces. Enter the front door into the entry, the first thing that you see is an immense staircase that just goes up and up and up. The flooring on the stairs, not marble, maybe a type of terracotta, are the newest thing in the house, only 400 years old. He has made apartments for tourists on the third and fourth floors. He got keys and started showing me empty flats.

The furnishings in the house, furniture, art, and objects d'art are all from the 14–15c. I am not kidding. It truly is a museum, possibly housing more original fine antiques than any one place in all of Europe. It's priceless. I would be afraid to sit on a sofa, drink out of the crystal or eat off of the china. The centre hall chandelier dates from 1392. The art work, priceless originals are beautiful but the frames, oh my goodness, who made those frames.

You also have to understand this is a very old house, well before electricity, so some of the wiring, while hidden by paint, shows and (new) all of the lights are on timers. I would think the electric bill is like the national debt. The house, because of the age and low voltage lighting, has an eerie feel about it. When he opened one door, leading to the attic, I had a feeling I was about to be thrown in and forgotten about. Yes, I have an active imagination, but it was eerie and I was in a strange country and felt as though I had walked through a mirror into generations of the far past. I was freaking myself out and with the lights being on short timers, I often found myself left in the dark on a staircase or in a room alone. It was just a bit scary.

Asking what was beyond one door on the second floor, he told me it was his papa's study, his papa having passed away years ago. He got the key to show me and when he opened the door, you took a step back in time. Everything in the room was exactly as his father had left it; the room was clean but the same papers remained on his desk, newspapers dating back to I think it said 1973 stacked on the floor, bookcases and bookcase, floor to ceiling on three walls lined and lined with leather bound and many first edition books. This room in itself is a museum.

Finishing the tour of the main house, we strolled into the garden and he showed me the motor court, the garage with stacks and stacks of firewood; heating the place must be a nightmare. There is a tower just passed the caretakers quarters called "Tower of Cassero." Solemn and austere, of the fourteenth c, Luigi says it is the spiritual epic of this blessed land of Lucignano. Past the tower is a smaller house that follows the trail of the gardens. The exterior of the house is beautiful and feels warm and cozy, but the interior has been abandoned and has fallen, unfortunately, to ruins.

The house, even though outside of the city, is a portion of the wall of the city. A heritage to be proud of. When leaving the estate, I found the iron gates, having been open, were now closed with a heavy chain and a padlock. I thought, for just a moment, that eerie feeling once again taking over that I was forever locked in this place. Wonderful or eerie? The lock was not engaged and I only had to unwrap the chain to leave.

If ever you are blessed enough to visit Lucignano, please visit Luigi and his wife, Antonella, give them my love and tell them *"vita in* wonderland." You can look this up on the internet, make reservations, and sweet sweet or maybe a bit of eerie dreaming while you are in the hands of this most enchanting *"museo storico."*

Via Rosini, 7—52046 Lucignano—Tele 0575 836260, www.ilcassero-tuscany.com

Truly an incredible city; be sure to visit the Gate of St. John, the Gate of St. Giusto, The Collegate Church with the true lamp of the history of the city, the beautiful churches filled with fine arts, the Sanctuary of our Land of the Querce, the Tower of the Nuns and of course the Tower of the Cassero.

# Naked in Tuscany

I am standing naked in central Tuscany, in Cortona. I am without all of the comforts life has afforded me. I am in a strange country, with a strange language and with customs not my own. I am in a land where church bells ring every hour of every day and where at 6:00 pm, all church bells ring, one right after the other.

I'm without my Mercedes, my house, my furniture, my clothes, my jewelry, nor do I have my shoes. I am without my family or my friends. My Rolex has been traded for a swatch. I live without appliances: dish-washer, trash-compactor, disposal, microwave; and I live without a bathtub. I do not have closets, dressers or nightstands. I have no desk on which to write my stories. I have no soft, warm carpets for my feet. I have no air, nor do I have central heat. I do not have a telephone but I have a camera. I have no yard, no garden, no space to call my own. I have two pair of jeans, one pair of dress pants and two skirts, but one is for summer. I have assorted shirts and sweaters, just a few. I have two pairs of shoes, enough underwear to not wash for a week. I have socks for one week, if it does not rain and ruin my socks. I have a blue jean jacket and a leather jacket. I have colorful scarves which I purchased here.

Winter is on its way and it is making me feel more naked, wondering if I can truly brave the cold that winter brings. Will my clothes freeze on the line? Will I truly be naked? I have never lived with so little, nor have I ever lived with so much happiness. But . . . *I miss my family and friends and wonder how my children can survive without me!*

# I've Been Dumped

All on my own, in Tuscany

I have been dumped, left on my own to find my way through Tuscany. No more car rides, traveling the wonderful back roads of this incredible world so far from home. No more Angiolo, no more Italian lessons. No more will Angiolo make funny faces and funny sounds trying to describe animals which I eat and wonder what I am eating: *Agnello, Capretto o Montone* or *Coniglio* (Lamb, Goat, Mutton or Rabbit). I especially loved his sounds and faces of a rabbit. He truly does not speak any English.

Yes, he wanted *"romantico"* and I did not, so we said our farewells and I am back on my own. But I forge ahead, traveling back on the buses and the trains. I think I prefer this but I will miss Angiolo.

I went to Siena for the wine tour and ended up having to spend the night, almost not finding a room and loving all of the mix-ups. I did find a room but it was after 8:00 pm and I was getting concerned. September is a big holiday month with travelers getting their last thrills before winter comes and scares them away. It's not the cold that frightens them into not visiting, it is the lack of efficient heat.

The vineyards are filled with the swollen grapes, ripening enough for harvest time. Harvest time is anywhere from mid September to mid October, depending on the rains. I think, if it rains too much the mold can set in, but it has only started afternoon showers in this, the last part of September.

The Chianti tour begins in Siena, four days a week, at two in the afternoon and lasting 4–6 hours. I wanted to go on this important tour before the grapes were picked, leaving the vines bare, with the grapes bursting with full maturity. Now, the grapes are large, heavy and pulling the vines down with their weight. These are beautiful grapes to make beautiful wines.

The tour includes the Chianti region: Castellina in Chianti, Radda in Chianti, Gaiole in Chianti, Panzano in Chianti, Meleto, Castello di Brolio, and the Gallo Nero (black cockerel) is the symbol of the Chianti Classico Consortium, all of the main villages of Chianti Classico wine region. You can sample, purchase and ship wines and listen to the pride of the estate owners. In Castellina in Chianti, there is a fifteenth C underground passage, built for defense purposes, and the *Enoteca Vini Gallo* Nero is a showcase for the region's wines.

If you have visited Napa Valley and fallen in love, you will not want to leave the Hearts of Chianti. I suggest a lifetime of being drunk on wine and staying forever. I learned, the wise have mastered finishing wine, cheese, oil and bread all at the same time, savoring that last bite with that last sip of wine.

It is amazing that Italians drink wine, all of the time, with every meal, dessert wines, coffee wines, grappa and *vin santo* and all other sorts but never, never will you see an Italian drink to the point of being drunk.

I will return later in the month to help pick grapes and again in December to pick the olives. I have arranged to pick grapes and olives close to home but I don't know if I get to stomp the grapes or not. My friends assure me they will make it possible, just for the fun of watching me. It is almost time to pick the figs and I want to help pick, I just want all of the experiences this wonderful Tuscany has to offer.

Today, I took the bus, then the train and went shopping in Arezzo. Waiting for my train leaving Arezzo, returning to Cortona, I met a young man named Giovanni (Johnny) from Romania. He spoke to me in Italian at the *stazione del treno*, asking if I enjoyed my day in Arezzo and to where was I returning. Not understanding exactly what he was saying, I replied, *"Parle a mi? Mi dispiace, io parlo poco Italiano."*

He said, *"Mi scusi,* I thought you were Italian."

Many people make the mistake of thinking I am *Italiana.* I find it enchanting and *molto complimento!* We rode the train together, he headed to Chuisi and I to Camucia.

I loved his stories of Romania and have invited him to Cortona next week. He was quizzing me about why I had not visited Romania in all of my travels. He told me of the mountains in the central and northern parts of his country and of the coast in the south.

He explained they were a democracy, an open country not to fear. He said there is no terrorism in Romania, no children with guns or bombs. It is a poor, proud country with people trying hard to make a living. Families were once large with 4–6 children, now the families have shrunk in size, most only having one child and some opting to have none.

Johnny is working in Italy to raise money to open a business in order to hire young men like himself. He hopes for marriage, a child and a happy life. He speaks five languages, his native language and the others learned in their school system. They start in primary school, at age 5, learning the languages of the world. Americans for the most part never understand the need for different languages until they are older, harder to learn, often not until adulthood. I learned more about Romania in my thirty minutes with Johnny than I ever learned in a history class. I am looking forward to our friendship.

Tomorrow I will take the train (alone) to visit Assisi and Perugia hoping to meet more people like Johnny.

Tonight I dined at *Osteria del Teatro* (the squealing of the wild boar), I had *Agnello* (Lamb chops) *con Spinaci con* pine nuts as the main course. But first I had barley and mushroom soup, filled with barley and topped with toasted bread and parmigiano and olive oil. For dessert I had a steaming pear with hot *cioccolato* sauce. To die for!

# Assisi

It took me days to get to Assisi, only an hour train ride away. First I was going with Angiolo but as you know, Angiolo dumped me. So, I decided to go it alone and take a train. I went to see Ivan, to ask about Assisi ,and he printed a train schedule for me. He said the best train to take was the 9:23 as it was a "*diretto*" and would only take an hour. The next train time for Assisi would be at 12:15 but that *treno* would not allow me enough time, I needed to catch the 3:20 back to Camucia or I would be spending another night out of town.

The bus schedule showed a 9:05 to Camucia, perfect for the 9:23 *treno* to Assisi. I got up early, got ready and went for my cappuccino and *pasta con crema*. At 8:30 I went to the *Tabaccheria*, to purchase my bus and train tickets. They were out of tren tickets and told me I would have to purchase it from the Information Agency. I went to the IA and it was *chiuso, non aperto* until 9:00 am. I had to catch the bus at 9:05 and could not wait. I decided, I would be an Italian "*vagabondo*," to take the train without a ticket, using my "*io no parlo Italiano*" to get me out of a fine, or so I was hoping. I waited and waited for the bus, now it was 9:20 and I knew I could not get the 9:23 train to Assisi.

I returned to the IA and purchased a ticket for the next day, hoping the bus would be on time to get me to the train station for the 9:23. The bus time worked out perfectly and I was in time for the train on my way to Assisi, finally!

I thought I had learned the train system well, but today I learned something new. The diretto, I thought meant it went directly to that place without stopping. That it is not what it means; we stopped at every little town. What it means is that is a direct train and you do not have to change trains. So I am thinking that the "*Regionale*" is the train that does not stop at every little place, maybe it only stops at one town in each region but it does not mean you will not have to change trains. I still have a great deal to learn.

Assisi is a walled town much like Cortona and when you get off of the train you must take a bus up to town centre. Getting off the train and seeing Assisi was all it took for me to fall in love with another hilltop town. It is magnificent! Sitting atop that hill, laid out like a long fortress, I couldn't wait to get on the bus, wanting to be on top of the mountain looking down on the immense valley. I found the perfect place on the northwestern slopes of Mt. Subasio (one of the mountains in the Apennine Chain), a hotel with a terrace overlooking the plain below, named after Spoleto, that extends up the hills to the city of Perugia, the Capitol of Umbria.

I have always heard of Tuscany, it is much talked about among Americans but I knew little of Umbria, an adjacent region to Tuscany. I have found Umbria to be every bit as glorious, beautiful and maybe even more historical than Tuscany. Umbria has its own wine regions, is know for olive oil and cheeses and the history is fascinating. As I sat at the hotel drinking cappuccino and photographing the valley, it dawned on me that I live here, in Italy.

Everyday, I wake up to Italians going to work, speaking their native tongue, their children walking in groups to school while singing and laughing. I take all of this for granted; it has become my life. It is almost surreal to think this is now my life. I am learning a new language, the Italian customs are becoming mine and I am learning the history of these magical hilltop *cittàs*.

The Italians speak of their hilltop *cittàs* as being "*molto* spiritual, and places of calm and tranquility," no truer words have been spoken. Life seems to slow down claiming a certain calmness we rarely (in our fast paced lives) seem to ever experience. This is the way of life for the persons living in Assisi and I felt it immediately upon my arrival.

The city of Assisi dates back to pre-Roman times. It was an important center, inhabited by the Umbri and then by the Romans. Assisi and St. Francis are one and the same thing. There is no other place where the spirit and the spirituality of the Saint are so omnipresent as Assisi. So many of the places speak of him, the little church of San Damiano, the Hermitage of the Carceri the cathedral of San Rufino, the hovel of Rivotorto, the Porziuncola, the basilica of Santa Chiara, the Bishop's palace, the Basilica complex erected in his honor. (1487) In the Lower Church of San Francesco, various silent witnesses are preserved which are tangible living signs of the Saint, historical documents that are part of his life: the Rule, the tunic, the blessing to Fra Leone written in his own hand. The parchment of the "blessing" is wrinkled and spotted because Fra Leone carried it on his person for 47 years, from 1224 to 1271, when on his deathbed he left it to the Holy Monastery.

The basilica complex of Assisi is famous the world over for its marvelous synthesis of architecture, painting and spirituality. It is the prototype of Italian Gothic art. Inside it houses the frescoes of the greatest painters of the thirteenth and fourteenth centuries. On September 26, 1997, there was a strong earthquake with violent tremors that tore the ancient and most sacred heart of the city of St. Francis. All of the main monuments, from the Cathedral of Saint Rufino to the Basilica of Saint Clare, from Santa Maria degli Angeli to the Sanctuary of Saint Damian, were seriously damaged and declared unfit for use.

The lost masterpieces of the frescos included sections of the famous Doctors' Vault, where St. Jerome was frescoed, and the section of the intrados of the counter-façade, where figures of St. Rufino, St. Anthony, St. Francis and St. Clare, all splendid frescoes by Giotto. Today you can still witness the devoted artists re-constructing the frescos, using the smallest pieces of mosaic tiles.

Assisi, known as 'The Blessed Town' because shortly before his death, as St. Francis was on his way to Santa Maria degle Angeli from Assisi, he stopped halfway down. Turning towards his city he blessed her with these words, "May you be blessed by God, holy city, 'for through you many souls will be saved and many servants of God will dwell in you and many of yours will be elected to the realm of eternal life.'"

# Perugia

He's back! Angiolo has returned! He says he has too much fun with me not to see the year out showing me and telling me of all of Italy. Yes, and I get my Italian lessons back!

Let's talk about Angiolo; he is a *mamonie*(a mama's boy). He has lived with his parents, in a castello in Cortona, his entire life. His mama cooks for him, cleans the casa, does the wash and arranges the entertainment.

How could he even consider *"romantico"* with me, or with anybody? Can you just imagine? Him bringing a "lady" home for the evening. Right, I would not want to see mama's face knowing I was spending the night with Angiolo in a casa he lives in with *lui's mamma e papà*.

Maybe, it was just a bit fun with our children sneaking boys and girls in through the windows when they were teenagers but really, at age 58 for him and 54 for me, the humor is just not there.

I am always playing with Angiolo, telling him he better *"telephono tu mama, tu es tardi and tu mama preparo tu mangerierie. Lei chuise the cucina, no mangerie per tu!"*

He laughs and says, *"Si, io sono un mammone e te sei una libera* American Lady."

He does tell me he has great respect for me traveling and living in another country, without knowing the language, without a car and without family. He says it is something he could not do. Even though he has traveled extensively, he is a *mammone* and must come home. New York City to him would mean immediate institutionalization, it would make him crazy.

Now my Italian is getting better, but I do still have large mix-ups. Angliolo ask me to go with him to Perugia and wanted to leave at 8:30. I told him, *"Impossibile andare a* 8:30, Mercado Mussolini (meaning Molesini) *consegnare* (to deliver) *mi mangerie alla* 9:00."

He said when he was en bano, barbering, he started laughing out loud about me saying Mussolini. When he came out of the *bagno*, his mamma asked why he was laughing. When he told her, she said, "*Tua donna americana è* pazza (crazy)."

So much for me wanting to meet mamma!

We finally agreed to leave for Perugia after my groceries were delivered. It is only about a 45 minute car ride but we kept detouring so he could show me *piccolo cittàs or piazzas* along the way. It is really wonderful having an Italian guide to travel with, without the restrictions of the train.

Perugia is the capital of Umbria, a large *città* with ancient history. There is the base citta, like Assisi, and center city is on top of the mountain. There is an underground parking facility with a sky mover to get you to "center city."

You actually enter the city inside the mountain which is the Vicolo della Rocca Paolina, the Paolina Fortress, named after Pope Paul III (Farnese), which was built on top of the ruins of the Baglioni Palaces. I think the original collapse of the city was due to the "Salt War" in 1540.

The "Salt War" was when the tax on salt brought the economy to a halt with many people suffering and not being able to sustain life. This salt tax is also why, even today, there is no salt used in the making of breads in Umbria and Tuscany, leaving the breads somewhat tasteless and only lasting for a day or so before becoming too hard to eat.

Perugia is a large city with shopping, cafés, restaurants, and hotels to accommodate the tourist. Besides being the capital it is also a large university city.

Priors' Palace, also known as the Town Hall, is an outstanding example of medieval architecture and is considered to be among the most elegant and famous in Italy. The Cathedral of St. Lawrence is a Gothic temple constructed between the 14c and 15c, although a large amount of the external facing remains incomplete.

Fontana Maggiore (The Great Fountain) stands in the central Piazza IV Novembre, the main tourist attraction and monumental heart of medieval Perugia. Looking out over the square are the Priors' Place, the Bishop's Palace and the Lawyers' Palace (Palazzo dei Notari), the side of the Cathedral and the Loggias of Braccio Fortebraccio. The fountain was built in 1275–78 and designed by Fra' Bevignate, assisted by Boninsegna da Venezia.

I found Perugia to be too big for a single day visit. Even with Angiolo being the perfect tour guide, I was losing much of the value of the city, finding myself confused and frustrated trying to understand his Italian and follow the history.

I found a perfect ancient old hotel, La Rosetta, in the heart of Perugia. I made reservation for October 16 for me and Quay. Another day in Perugia! And tomorrow, weather permitted, we are off to visit Gubbio!

# Is There a "Farmer" in Me?

I was raised in the city, or cities; New York, Boston, Chicago and just before I reached 18, I moved to Europe for five years and later moved to Dallas. My maternal grandparents had a ranch in Texas, where on most long holidays and every summer I would visit. So I do have country in me.

I learned at a young age, four or five, how to stand on a chair, reaching the wall phone to call my grandmother. I would tell her that she had better come see about me because I may not be okay. My grandparents would take the train, never flying, for that long two day and a night journey to come see about me. I was a bit spoiled by them; spending my vacations with them was like living in fairyland, always going to Dallas or Waco shopping, learning, at age five to shop for my lace panties at Neiman's or Cox's, and saying, "Just charge that to Mrs. Fred Archer."

I often wondered how my grandparents ever came together. My grandmother was all city and my grandfather was all country. She was always in church and having the preacher to Sunday lunch once a month, while my grandfather was taming the wild.

I never thought much about the ranch, growing crops and animals running wild. I can remember sitting on the wrap-around porch in the evenings with my grandfather cupping his mouth and saying something like "sug, sug, sug," winking at me and telling me he was calling the cattle up to eat. After about five minutes of him doing "his calling," the cattle (black angus) would come up over the hills, herds and herds of them, looking like chocolate pudding cascading down the hillside. Watching him sit in his rocking chair, calling his beloved cows, didn't look like much work to me.

I took the orchards, the crops and the animals for granted. I never gave thought to how any of it survived or grew. It was just there and it seemed to make everyone around happy.

Now, I find myself living in Tuscany, in the middle of one of the largest farmlands in the world. Yes, I do live in a town but we are totally surrounded by the farmlands. My eyes are wide open and my grandfather would be proud; I now see what farming is truly about.

For the first time in my life, I feel the "love" of the farmers and I am becoming one of them. I picked grapes! It is grape harvest in Tuscany and the vast population is out picking grapes.

I had dreamed about being a part of this grape harvest, wanting to pick them, eat them, stomp them and drink the wines from the very grapes I picked. Well, I lasted four hours, thanks to the great sky opening up and showering us with sheets of rain. I didn't exactly pray for the rain but I was wishing for that downpour.

Picking grapes is not an easy task. I was dressed with rubber boots, my hair tied back with a scarf (to catch the sweat), a straw hat and cute little gloves with the fingers cut out. I thought all of this very exciting and I was ready to harvest those grapes. No one told me how hard it was going to be, that I would be walking up or down hills, that my back would hurt from bending over, that my shoulders would start aching, nor that my stained finger tips would start burning. It's painful to pick these grapes. As I would fill up my straw basket filled with the heaviness of my bunches of grapes, I would wonder how I would manage carrying my basket to the large container on wheels. Every basket load got heavier and heavier.

I took a fast peek at my watch, knowing I had been working for hours, and only a mere forty minutes had passed. I was in for a very long day! Forty minutes, how could it only be forty minutes, surely the day is almost over. I looked around, everyone was busy, no one seemed to be tired or in pain. There was no way I was going to tell anyone I was tired and wanted to go home. This grape picking is serious business and besides being laughed at, run out of town or shot, no one would appreciate having to stop their picking to take me back to town. I was forced to be brave and to be strong, but I knew what was really going to happen; I was going to die from being overworked.

I was given a stick with a knot on the end of it as part of my picking gear. When I asked what it was for, they said to use it if I came across one of the little "vipers." When I first got to the vineyard, I looked everywhere for the "vipers" even imagining they would be coiled around the vines but as the day wore on and I grew more tired, I was hoping one might bite me and put me out of my misery.

Was that thunder? I thought. "I heard thunder," I told my fellow picker.

He said, "*Niente, un pò di pioggia* won't hurt us."

But, thank you, the sky opened up and here the downpour began. It came in sheets making it impossible to see or to hear. I watched as everyone started to leave the fields and knew there was a god and I was being rescued.

I rode in the back of a pickup to town holding on to my "bounty" of grapes, ones I got to take home with me. I was drenched but felt great that I pulled this "grape picking" off without anyone knowing I was a big baby just wanting to go home.

At the end of picking there will be a big sagra, which I will have the honor of attending because I didn't stop working, the rains came to save my day.

On this big beautiful farm, reaching from coast to coast, we have more crops and game to feed on than I ever imagined. Not just the grapes, there are chestnut trees. Some of the chestnut trees are not good for us, only for the animals; I cannot yet tell the difference in the trees. I am amazed to learn all of the uses for chestnuts. I must do a story on just the chestnuts and how they saved the Italians from starvation during the war. They also have figs trees, olive trees, bushes with great large capers, mushrooms and truffles. The wild boar roam the hills at night and you can hear them along with the fox. The white longhorn cows (*Chianina*) roam free on the ranges mixing with the sheep and goats.

I think back to my first arriving in Cortona and having a toothache, talking with Jamie and commenting on people's teeth. He had said to me that we live in a farming community, they think of their crops, not of their teeth. Now I feel ashamed that I would have ever said something so snotty. These are my people, my fellow farmers. I am proud of them and thankful to them for all of the foods I love eating and the wines I love drinking. Bless you my fellow farmers, and yes, I think there is a little "farmer" in me.

# Communism

I don't live in a grand villa outside of town. I don't have a fireplace in every room nor do I have electric central heat in which to stay warm.

I live in an empty building with stone walls, brick floors and brick ceilings. I do have a fireplace but it was blocked up, years ago. My building is over 500 years old, well before insulation was used. I have concrete steps, uneven with the risers not all being the same size, with narrow stairwells and drafty windows. There are no occupied apartments above, below or beside my apartment to help me stay warm. My heat will be the only heat in the entire building.

My pleasure has been to enjoy the best parts of spring, summer and fall and now winter is well on its way. With the rain and the wind, I am not sure there is a best part of winter for my enjoyment. I don't think I have enough Italian blood to keep me warm in this, the approaching winter.

Cortona is one of the prettiest places I have ever lived and there are many things I dearly love. I love the age and the history of the *città*. I love the people and their kindness and their openness. I love how they have carved out the stone in the lower parts of the buildings to make room for more stores and shoppes. I love the miles of partaire going along the walls of Cortona. The partaire, at any time is filled with people walking and children playing. It has its own outdoor theater, fountain, benches and the view of the valley and lake Trasimeno.

Cortona has taught me to live with less and find more enjoyment in everyday life and in finding the hearts and souls of the people. It allows for people, from all over the world, to make this their home and feel a part of this world.

The Cortonese are anxious to teach their ways, their languages and to share their lives with all that find their way into this charming Eden. They are truly interested in us, the *stranieri*, and care about us and will do anything to help us find the total enjoyment of Cortona.

Today the weather is called "*brutto tempo*"! Meaning it's ugly, rainy, windy, damp and cold. Even though it is "*brutto tempo*" and I needed an umbrella all day, I stayed out. I needed the people. I needed their body heat and warm food and drink.

I returned to my apartment after dinner and there is no way to express the coldness, the dampness, the misery in my apartment. I have to have heat! I have to have heat now! I turned my register as high as it goes, 30, turned on the oven to start the warming process until the radiators began heating. I waited and I waited, for two hours. The radiators remained cold, yielding no heat, no warmth. Something is wrong with my heaters. It's night and there is no way anyone will come to fix my heaters. I do not have a home number for my *immobiliario* or my super.

I finally called my American friend, Donna; she has a fireplace, a working fireplace. I told her what was going on with my heat and asked for any suggestions.

There is no way anyone would believe what Donna told me. She said that the city decides when to turn on the heat for apartments, houses and businesses; the people can't regulate their own. There will be no heat in Cortona until November, not even the first of November; it will be the last of November.

This can't possibly be true. What about the babies, what about the old, what about me? This is communism!

# Polizia! Polizia! Carabinieri!
## Mi puo aiutare!

There are so many different types of police in Italy, when in need, you never know where to turn or whom to call. I never thought I would need the *polizia* or the *carabinieri* in Cortona but I never imagine many things I may need.

There are the tax police, they rule Italy. If you are in a bar, a restaurant, shoppe or at the dentist or doctor, after paying you will be given a receipt. Keep the receipt because if you are stopped leaving the establishment without the receipt, you will be fined and the owner will be fined. Now, I have never actually been stopped but the shoppe owners warn you constantly about keeping your receipt.

If you want to pay cash for something, under the table (so to speak), you will get a large discount and no receipt. The shoppe owner or dentist or doctor will tell you to say services are not complete and you will be paying at time of completion.

A lady from England bought an apartment just off the main square and was thrilled that the apartment had a large terrace, rarely found with an apartment in Cortona. The terrace was the deciding factor in choosing that particular apartment. Sale completed, she immediately began an expensive endeavor of having an arbor built, the floor tiled, and filling her terrace with potted plants (no small feat getting those heavy pots and plants to a fourth floor terrace). Just about the time the work was completed and paid for, now arrived another type of *polizia*, telling her this renovation is not allowed and must immediately be taken away. She was so angry, and finally realizing she had absolutely no say in the matter, she tore it all down (herself, in her rage), and left it piled in the middle of the terrace. It remains there today, some six months later. I guess there is no police to police the mess on the terraces and there are many. Are the priorities right?

Now, I have another friend, Carol, who has opened a bed and breakfast in the building next to mine. She got busy decorating, wanting a very welcoming exterior for possible guests. She put in window boxes and painted the shutters red. She has a four story building offering many shutters. At the completion of painting the shutters, here come the *polizia* to tell her she could not have red shutters and they must return back to brown immediately or she will receive a considerable fine. All shutters in Cortona must be brown or green or a natural wood. It's not even a pretty brown.

My questions is: with Cortona being an extremely small town with *polizia* everywhere, on every corner, walking around and driving the city at all times of the night and day, why oh why, did they not inform her of the paint rule during the week and a half it took to have the darn things painted?

There is really no crime in Cortona, no Italian ever drinks to the point of becoming intoxicated, the kids are too well behaved, the tourists don't steal and no one has guns, little or no crime. However, just after being in Cortona three weeks, I was out one night, sitting with friends at a table on Via Nationale when screaming down the street came about fifty *polizia* cars, police everywhere! I wanted to hide under the table, having no idea what was happening. I almost thought it another planned festival, but no! It was a drug raid. Oh *mio Dio*, a drug raid in Cortona! Come to find out there had been a three month investigation going on between the *polizia* of Cortona, Arezzo, Roma and Naples. Over seventy people where arrested and lots of drugs confiscated. But it still remains a fact that there is little to no crime in Cortona.

Many months later I found myself in the need of the *polizia* or the *carabinieri*. I live in an empty building that is four stories. There is an apartment on each floor, mine being on the third floor, and even the upstairs attic space has been finished out for holiday rentals.

Now, each of the apartments have for a week or two at a time been rented to a tourist, usually a couple but sometimes many people have occupied one of the apartments. And at times, the vacant apartments have been used as love nests for a couple of hours at a time. The noise has never been disruptive and I have had no reason to complain. Well, not until a few weeks ago. It was a Saturday night about midnight when

I returned to my apartment and the noise above me sounded as though someone was using the floor as a *bocci* court, can you imagine, metal balls rolling on a brick floor? Thankfully, I was tired, the noise did not continue for a long time and I was able to fall asleep.

The next day I ran into Roberto (my *immobiliario*) and asked him about the noise. He said maybe they had rented the apartment and the new tenants were moving in or re-arranging the furniture. Made perfect sense to me but during the following week, I never heard anyone or saw anyone.

The next Saturday night, I had stayed in for the night, about 9:00 the noise began. I heard the downstairs building door open, about four or five people started upstairs, passing my door, laughing and carrying boom boxes with loud Italian music already playing. About every five or ten minutes the downstairs bell would ring, the apartment upstairs would allow entry and more footsteps were heard on the concrete stairs. This procession of people continued for a long time.

Let the party begin. Oh my, will I have to listen to this all night! About 11:00, I wanted to go to bed, even thought perhaps it might be a little quieter in the bedroom, but oh no, it sounded as though they would come through the floor at any moment.

I decided to be a big person, a nice person, to knock on their door and ask them politely to please stop the noise. I did this three times, to no avail. They would not open their door to talk to me, just yell through the door and the last time, I think they said something very rude about "american lady." I had had enough and it was time to call the *polizia* or the *caribiniere*, I didn't know which one to call but I was calling someone!

The *polizia* station is at the end of my street, a two minute walk or a 30 second drive. I called the *polizia,* 112, got Camucia and was told they would patch me through to Cortona. The Cortona *polizia* dispatcher did not speak English and had not a clue as to what I was saying. I ended up calling Peter to call the *polizia* and have them come immediately; by now, I was mad.

It took the *polizia* 45 minutes to get to my house (glad it was not an emergency) and even though the *polizia* rang the bell for upstairs, the intercom was not answered. The *polizia* announced themselves but were not allowed entry. I leaned out my window to talk to the *polizia* who informed me he had not been allowed entry and could not open the *porta* (door). Now of course my intercom had never been repaired (job too piccolo) so I had to run down stairs in my pj's to open the door.

It turns out the son of the owner of the apartment had been sneaking the key and inviting all of his friends for "big" parties on Saturday nights. No more partying for those kids! Not in my building anyhow.

But in the defense of these Italians kids, I must say, they all apologized to me as they were leaving, there was no alcohol nor were there any drugs. They are polite and well behaved just looking for a place to hang out and listen to their music. I almost wanted to tell them to continue to party but honestly, I like my sleep.

# A Day in my Life in Cortona

I never walk twenty steps from my front door before someone says, "*buongiorno*" or "*buonasera, come va?*" Rarely, do I get to Via Nazionale or Piazza Repubblica before someone has walked up behind me, linked their arm in mine and said "coffee." Now, when I first got to Cortona and someone would walk up and say "coffee," I didn't know if they were asking me to have coffee, if they thought my name coffee, if they were asking if I had had coffee or if I like coffee. But they quickly led me to a table or in *il bar* and started ordering, so we were having coffee.

When living in the states, I found I always had to plan my day. Primarily because it had to often correspond with other people's plans and driving a car. Even the simplest things had to be considered. If having lunch with a friend, you had decide where, when, is there convenient parking, do they have a smoking area, is service fast or slow and will it fit in to the time we have allowed. It takes a great deal of planning for something so simple.

Not so in Cortona, I practically never make plans. Only so if I want to see someone for a special reason, or am planning a day of travel or in my case, time to write. Yesterday was one of my (sort of) planned days because I wanted to write and I had called Amy to meet me at 4:00 for a three hour visit. Giovanni had a tour lasting until 7:00, so Amy could take the bus up and hitch a ride back with him.

Angiolo and I had taken Amy and Giovanni to dinner Monday evening to celebrate them expecting a baby. They had been trying for several months and had found out that very day "baby was on the way." When you have dinner with Italian men they dominate the conversations and Amy and I found we needed more time together and arranged to meet later in the week (Thursday). I always start my day at Caffè La Saletta for my warm *pasta con creama* and cappuccino.

When I first moved here, I would go to Bar degli Artisti for breakfast and sometimes even for lunch; I was an excellent client and they got lots of my euros. Bathrooms in Italy, especially in tourist towns, are firmly restricted to patrons, signs are even posted.

"L'uso del bagno e'riservato ai soli clienti del bar, grazie!"

One day I found myself in need of a bathroom, couldn't wait, and walked into a Bar, used the bathroom and when I was walking out the owner's wife started yelling at me in Italian, following me out in the street, still yelling for me not to use their bathroom. I was so embarrassed. Valentino De Luca had always been my waiter and tried to explain to her that I was a valued customer but she wasn't hearing him, just bent on me knowing not to ever use their bathroom. So that il bar gets no more of my euros.

Let's talk about bathrooms in Italy, in Europe. I consider myself very lucky to live in Cortona; the bathrooms are probably as clean and nice as you will ever find in Italy. The only thing I had to get used to is the bathrooms are for men and women. Normally there are two separate rooms, one for the sink and unlike the states, no stall, a completely separate room with the toilet. The toilets have both a seat and a lid. I have walked out of the toilet room, numerous times, to find a man standing there washing his hands, I only hope that he didn't pee in the sink.

Now, in other parts you will find baths ranging from fairly clean to "make you throw up" filthy. Traveling on the *autostrade* the range goes from very bad to unbelievable. In more remote areas you will find no lid, no seat and often only a hole in the floor. Hope your knees are good because it is bend, stoop, balance and hope for the best. At one place I went there was a hole in the floor, a metal grate covering the floor with running water under the grate. I went in to pee and came out throwing up . . . yuck! You also learn to carry your own toilet paper!

I left my apartment at nine and headed for coffee. About half-way there, Vivienne slipped her arm in mine and said, "Coffee." Sure why not. On the way, Enzo stuck his head out of his shoppe and told me the new arrival was in from Max Mara and I told him I would stop by after coffee. On the way to Enzo, Nunccio came out for a morning two cheek kiss and said Sabrina could do my hair today, if I had time.

So now I was shopping, visiting with Vivienne and getting my hair done. No plans for my day!

I have always read about Italians doing a three-kiss on the cheek when meeting someone or leaving. I have never had that three-kiss action, I have only had one on each cheek but I do have those wonderful two-cheek kisses about twenty times a day. I love the Italians. We have coffee, shop at Enzos; actually I was just going to take a peek at the new arrivals and not shop.

Well, I shopped! Ever since the "cold" front we had a few weeks ago I had been thinking I needed a really heavy winter coat. It was easy to put off once the weather had turned warm again, about 70 or 26. I was even worried that I might be guilty of putting it off until all of the better coats in Cortona had been sold. Enzo had the perfect coat for me but the cost, oh my! He had just gotten in a beautiful Moncler, in purple or dark grape. A three-quarter length, quilted, down filled, hooded and very light and of course a perfect fit. I had to have it, at the dear cost of 435 euro's. I would be warm for the winter. I also bought two pair of Max Mara pants but he discounted everything, saying I was a good customer, making me feel good but it was *"molto caro."* Then I was off to have my hair done.

After my hair was done, I knew if I was going to write anything I needed to go directly to my apartment; but no, there was Giorgio (a local artist) and he had to have coffee and visit with me. Off we went to the Fusion Bar, sat outside to have a coffee which went into lunch.

Across the street from the Fusion is the Antichità Cortona, an antique store with beautiful furniture; every morning the owner brings out display pieces usually with the help of Massimo. Like most days he was outside polishing his furniture with a brush and oil.

He began singing Italian Opera, O *so-o-ole Mi-i-io* rang out in the street and suddenly he walked the five steps over to me and said that I was a lovely lady and inspired him to sing from his heart and that this opera was for me; only in Italy!

Having lunch with Giorgio left me no time for writing but I still had a couple of hours before meeting Amy and enough time to go to the I-net bar. The I-net bar is operated by Valentino de Luca's mother, Florica (Fiorella) Costachi, a lady I dearly love and they live on my street, so we have become good friends. I use to go to the bar, read, write and send stories and get out; it cost 1 euro for fifteen minutes, so we all learn not to dally.

Now, I always spend time talking and having an espresso and my kisses and hugs and now, no matter how long I stay it only cost me 1 euro. I love friendship the Italian way. Also, no one at the bar speaks English even though all of the clientele is English speaking. I love the signs in the bar. There is one that says (for cost of) "pays computer" and list the prices and if one of the computers is out of order there will be a sign posted "Break" instead of broken or out of order.

The cobblestone streets in Cortona are so hard on shoes and luck would have it, leaving the I-Bar, the front sole of my shoe separated. I sat down on the step in the piazza to see if I could get the glue to stick enough to get me home without the flip flop of the lose sole. Angiolo came up to see if there was a problem and when I showed him, he told me to hop in his car and he would take me to get it fixed. I thought he was taking me somewhere in Cortona but he drove out of the walls of Cortona on to the winding back roads and I had no idea where we were headed. I told him I had to return by 4:00 to meet Amy.

Angiolo had been in Florence earlier in the day and, as promised, he had printed out the train schedules for my travel to meet Quay in Roma, and for us to return going to Orvieto and on to Peruguia and Assisi. He had the schedules in his backseat and he pulled over to the side of the road, on a very high up cliff (my side) with crazy Italian drivers speeding by. He took out his yellow magic marker and began reviewing the schedules with me, planning my trip. I told him we really didn't have to do this right now, the trip still being two weeks away but he would have it no other way. Since his retirement he has become the *vagabondo però organizzato! Andiamo, per favore, io devo Ritornare Cortona alle 4!*

We continued the drive down the winding roads, leaving Cortona, passing Ossaia and coming up on to Terontalo where he took a left into a residential area. He stopped at an apartment with a garage, the garage door being open and walla, a shoe repairman.

Here sat an aging portly man dressed in a leather apron repairing shoes. He has been repairing shoes for 61 years. He was seated in a chair, wobbly and squeaking at his every move; I knew it was going to break at any moment. There was an old table in front of him covered in lacquer, polish, dyes and glues with every sort of tool imaginable. He took my shoe, ground it with a machine, re-glued it and said, "Sit, have a coffee while it dries." I tried to pay him but he wouldn't take my money.

On the way back to Cortona we passed a sign that said "*Ape con Miele*" and I asked Angiolo if we could stop. I had learned the word ape one day while having lunch with Amy and Giovanni at a sidewalk caffé. It's a bee and is pronounced apa! We had a bee flying around our table, Amy was so freaked out and Giovanni said, "Ah, to get rid of marriage, just bring home a bag of apes." He meant to say bees. The word took hold and is now part of my limited Italian vocabulary. I also knew the word *Miele* (honey) from my trip to Pienza. So the sign said Bee with Honey. We stopped and visited with the bee farmer who was covered head to toe with astronaut looking gear while tending to his bees. It takes a lot of work for the honey. But after my grape picking, I knew not to offer my help.

Angiolo got me to the bus stop in Cortona just as Amy was arriving, we said our goodbyes, *ciao, a più tardi* and Amy and I were off for prosecco. We had only been seated a few minutes when Donna (Donatella) joined us, then Diana came and Katerina came by to visit; we were a full house of Goddesses di Cortona. We had dinner and then a long walk on the partaire before Amy left and the group split up. Donna and I remained together and went to visit Mara at the Brasilian restaurant.

I had been trying for days to get back with Mara to finalize our plans for me to visit Brazil. I think we finally decided on me arriving in January and returning to Cortona with her in February. Around 10:00 a friend of Mara's from Roma showed up. His name I think is Riccardo; we did trade phone numbers but I may have gotten confused and put the wrong name in my cell phone as I now have two Riccardo's listed in my phone.

I told him that I would be visiting Roma in two weeks to meet my friend from the states. He has offered to be our tour guide in his car while we are in Roma. He has a villa just outside the walls of Cortona and a home in Roma. He is a great looking man, tall, with good teeth, and a great fit (oh no, that was my coat) and he is returning to Cortona next week to take me out. I can't wait.

It is now after midnight and I bid my goodbyes and am off to mi casa and the bed.

I had another long and unplanned day. Just as I crawl into bed, my phone rang. It was Peter wanting to know if I was still in town and wanted to have a glass of *vino*. Oh, no Peter, I've just gone to bed.
*BUONANOTTE!*

# Inverno is Coming

There is not an Italian that will tell you that September is a winter month, but I am telling you, it is late September, 6:30 pm, damp and cold, and I'm thinking this is winter. I know I am in serious trouble.

The Italians never turn on the heat until late October or early November; I need mine now. My socks will no longer last me a week. I'm wearing two pair at a time. My clothes are not drying on the line, about the time they are just barely damp it starts to rain. I so need a dryer. I had to iron a pair of pants dry this morning just to have something to wear. Gas is what is used to heat the *casas;* we have little things on the wall, maybe it is like a furnace, one in every room. It is controlled with a thermostat on the wall. They say I am lucky in my apartment as I am hooked to the city gas while many people have to take these tanks and have them filled with gas. The cost of my gas is half the price of theirs but still *molto, molto caro.*

They tell me to never raise my thermostat higher than 18c and at that my monthly bill should be around 400euros ($480). But hey, 18c is only about 66 f, and what kind of heat is that? I won't even be able to get out of my bed at that temperature. And I don't have a nice hot bubble bath to warm me. They also told be to be patient, that with the stone walls, brick floors and brick ceilings, as the apartment will take a long time to heat. I think what they really mean is it is not going to heat up until summers rolls around!

When I first moved in, I moved the kitchen table over by the window to get the light while writing; now I am going to have to move it back, just between the wall heater and the oven.

I need sweatpants, wool knee socks, thermal underwear, a down parka, and one of those wool caps with the face and that will just be for in the house. I have no clue what is required for outdoors. I bought a pair of knee high boats today with rubber soles; I think I will wear these as house shoes. I bought a down comforter. I have two quilts and my comforter on my bed and that is the warmest place I can find in the house. Will I have to spend my winter in bed? I so dread taking a shower.

It was just too cold and damp to go for my prosecco. I am going to have to find a warm alcoholic drink for the winter. Knowing I have to go out at 8:00 to eat is enough of a challenge for me. Maybe I need to get things to keep in the house, like food, for the winter.

I am dressing in tights, socks, jeans, and undershirt, a sweater then a pullover and a jacket, gloves and a scarf around my neck with my knee high boots to go to dinner. The Italians are already laughing at me; after all, *inverno* (winter) is just coming; it's not here yet!

# Vita in Italia

Rest assured, I was standing at my *immobiliario's* office early the next morning to find out about the heat, my heat. Yes, it is true; there is a city "ordinance" that controls the usage of heat or gas. Roberto explained to me this is an old ordinance, not completely enforced but one could still be subject to a fine, possibility a hefty fine. A fine does not matter to me, I just want heat when I want heat.

In order for the radiators to work, something must be done with the water closet, which Roberto has ordered done. I don't know how long it will take but the service, I am assured, has been ordered. There is also a possibility that when this has been done, it will be reported to the polizia in charge of these matters.

Now, I jest when I say this is communism. Possibly, it is the best way to make sure we are all aware of the resources we use and will not cause abuse. I am in a country, in a town, where they can and do run out of resources like gas, and abuse is something we are all guilty of, thinking there is always plenty of everything. Not so, and we should be more aware.

We live with the same restrictions at home, we have just become more tolerant. Case in point, I just received, per my daughter, a letter indicating I must change the color of my front door back to its original color. It appears I did not get permission from the Home Owner's Association to paint my door a different color. Now I am subject to a fine.

*Il tempo* in Italia has once again become warm; today I woke up to 12c or about 55 and the high will be 17c or 63, all very doable for me. To make things even better, there is no rain or piove. I am still very glad that I bought my new winter coat.

I woke up very early this morning, something I have not done for a long time. It was only 5:00 am but I thought coffee and an early start would be fun. I switched on the TV, thinking there might be something in English, but no, no English. However, if I was into some erotica,

I had my choice of Lesbo Vivo or Racconti Erotici, all for free. I am assuming Italian children never wake early. All of this was for free but I have to pay extra for CNN. There was a Russian weather station, the weather girl being topless!

Where are the *Polizia?*

Angiolo and I continue to travel the back roads finding the smallest of hilltop towns with interest. Yesterday, we found two. Actually, Angiolo, as he says, visited them on TV and thought they may be of interest to me.

The first was a tiny village, *nome Monte del Lago*, situated high up and on the very tip of Lago Trasimeno. The first obvious thing was that one casa or villa dominated the entire town. The villa was at the highest point with vast *"il giardino"* with an immense stone wall encompassing the entire property. It appeared to be a small fishing village with several residential buildings and small shops servicing only the town without thought of tourists.

The next hilltop town near Perugia was Solomeo. If I thought one villa dominated Monte del Lago, I did not understand what domination could be. On the drive up the hill of Solomeo, a grand and vast property, garden and villa is all one can see, immediately fooled into thinking it is the town itself. It was hard to determine how many stories the villa rose to, as you only get glimpses of the villa itself. The villa rest on the top of the hill with the town just steps below. The villa is the only residence of wealth, all else pales in comparison.

There is a small B&B and one other small, two-story casa, one church and one il bar. Several other residential buildings, very well maintained, house the many employees of the one factory and the retail shop.

I felt as though I had entered the town from Stepford Wives; it was obvious the man in the villa owned the entire town. Solomeo is a manufacturing town, producing first the material, then the weaving of the material into sweaters and pullovers and selling their wares in their own store and shipping to stores all over Italy, maybe all over the world.

This man loves his town; he has built beautiful parks, and piazzas with fountains, and has brick paved almost the entire city.

We found only two stores in the town. One being the store of sweaters, in every color, style and size. The other was *il bar*, which was the coffee bar, *tabacchi* shop, *supermercato,* deli, restaurant and meat store, all in a mere 1000 sq. ft. That was it, the rest of the town were buildings housing factories producing the sweaters.

We took pictures, great sites of ancient buildings adjacent to the new construction, probably more factories for production; the town is the largest producer of sweaters in all of Italy.

We grabbed sandwiches and cokes at the "all in one" store and enjoyed a picnic at the beautiful, brick-paved piazza, next to the wall fountains. We were absolutely the only visitors in town. We returned late, about 8:30 from our adventure.

Being tired I went directly to my own modest casa. On the way, I stopped by to see Mara. She wanted to let me know that Alessandro had been trying, all day, to find me. My phone had been out of range, it usually is out of range, and his calls had not come through.

Now, you might be wondering who is Alessandro? He is who I thought was Riccardo. How I got Riccardo, and now having two Riccardo's saved on my phone, is a true mystery. I am having too much wine, too much prosecco, or just too much fun!

Anyhow, I now have a dinner date with Alessandro Friday night. This should be interesting if I don't get ill, throw up (the thought of dating makes me do that) and have to cancel the date. We shall see.

# Ceramica di Cortona
### Terrecotte Tradizionali
### di
### Giulio Lucarini

If ever there is an artist, a true artist, he will share, teach and train his love, his art and his life. Giuseppe Marconi was just that artist, that rare person that shared and taught the love of his life, the love of his *ceramica*. Unfortunately, he passed away in 1986 at the age of ninety. However, his legacy did not die. His love of *ceramica* was passed on to Giulio Lucarini who not only was so gracious to show me his life but to tell me of his love and respect for Giuseppe Marconi. Giulio has sculptured a bust of Giuseppe, his teacher, his mentor and has it proudly sitting on a shelf in his laboratory next to a bust he has done of his fourteen-year-old son.

Giulio and his wife, Antonella Fazzini, own the ceramica shoppe in Cortona on Via Nazionale, 54. Giulio trained under Giuseppe twenty-five years ago and has shared his art and love of ceramica with the people and the visitors of Cortona since 1980.

Giulio's *laboratorio* is located at Vicolo Vagnucci 3, in an alleyway or small strada attached to the back of his shoppe. The *laboratorio* standing two stories with his ovens, his tools and his beautiful creations.

They were gracious enough to not only let me into their lives but to take me through the steps of their craft and allow me to tour the *laboratorio*. The process or system used in the making of the *ceramica* is called *Sigillata*. The *Sigillata* is the pure part of the clay while the Rena is the grit. The clay is placed in pots of water and allowed to—with stirring—separate, the Rena settling to the bottom and the *Sigillata* rising to the top. The clay needs this purity, the *Sigellata*, so as not to cause crackling. The glazing process contains no lead.

There were many pots of clay resting in their water baths throughout the *laboratorio* and I noticed all of them were of different colors: pastel greens, terracottas, various shades of gray and white. I asked, showing my total ignorance, if dye had been added. Giulio explained to me that he "hunted" his clays in woods, country, valleys and mountainsides in the areas of Cortona, finding the perfect clays with the perfect colors. He would then dig these clays up and bring them to his *laboratorio* to create his magic.

Magic is truly what Giulio creates in his modest workshop. Not only did I tour but Giulio decided the best way to explain the process was to show me the process. He donned his gloves, wetted his clay and began a fast kneading process. He separated the piece of clay three times, rolled it in a ball, turned away from me, saying it would cause splatter, and smacked it several times. He then turned on his wheel and when it began spinning, he wetted it with water, sat his clay and began creating. Within minutes his creation began appearing, rising and cresting, forming the perfect shape. Within fifteen minutes his simple lump of clay became a masterpiece, a perfect vase. I was so fascinated by the process, I almost want lessons.

While in Cortona make a visit to their lovely shoppe filled with *ceramica*, the design of course, is the beautiful sunflower of Tuscany. If you are not coming soon for a visit, share the experience on their website, www.cortonaweb.net.

If traveling, in the future, their nineteen-year old daughter, after finishing school, plans on opening a shoppe in New York City to continue this wonderful part of history.

With love and appreciation, this writing is for Giulio Lucarini and Antonella Fazzini and their family.

# Forever Friends

As we adults reach that dreaded middle age, it suddenly occurs to all of us that we have acquired many, many, many acquaintances but have only a handful of "forever friends." I am so fortunate for my "forever friends" and now, living in Cortona, I have even added to that handful.

One of my best "forever friends" (from Texas) came for a visit on my birthday. We met in Rome, at the airport. The airport in Rome is very large, always bustling with people arriving or departing or there to meet someone, armed guards, shop owners and then there was me, looking for Quay. I knew before taking the train from Cortona to the Rome airport that at best it was going to be difficult for us to find one another. I had warned Quay not to move from where she exited her gate and if I was late, due to the numerous train strikes, to be patient and wait. We both knew if we absolutely could not connect we could go our separate ways to the hotel and meet there, but we were still hopeful.

When I got off the train and entered the airport, it was as if the seas had parted. I went directly in the direction of the gate; there were no people and Quay was descending the escalator, the only person on the escalator, and there we were face to face. Can you imagine the luck!

Before we could even exit the door, there was a taxi driver taking our luggage and guiding us to the cab. We were whisked away to our hotel. Life should always be so simple; he even let me smoke in his cab!

The hotel was perfect, one of the most beautiful hotels in Rome, thank you Jerry and Quay for those wonderful Starwood points (please, buy another unit and get more points for next year). I should be in Portugal by then and I know it will inspire another visit. The location was perfect for a walk to *Piazza di Spagna* (The Spanish Steps) and *Fontana di Trevi* (Trevi Fountain), so off we went for the best birthday of my life. Actually, it was the second best. The first was in Hawaii with George and him giving me an incredibly big beautiful diamond wedding ring for my birthday. Love you George, another "forever friend."

The next day, at Alessandro's insistence, he gave us a perfect guided tour of the best spots in Rome. He may rank one of my "forever friends." Who would ever offer to tour anyone, in a car, all over Rome. It was wild riding in his car from place to place, crazy Italian drivers, no apparent lanes and at breath taking speeds . . . did we really survive that! In one piece and happy at the end of the day and with all of the walking, we fell into bed.

We headed, by train, to Orvieto for the day. Orvieto is in between Rome and Cortona and a town I knew Quay would not want to miss. I wanted to share as much of my beloved Italy without backtracking so we had to stop in Orvieto on the way to Cortona, meaning we had our luggage with us. Because of terrorist threats Italy has taken all of the lockers out of the train stations. We were stuck with rolling our bags around Orvieto.

Thankfully the town is not as hilly as Cortona but after a day there we were exhausted and thrilled to be back on the train to Cortona.

I called Angiolo on our way to Cortona, told him the time of our arrival and he picked us up at the train station in Camucia and took us up the hill to Cortona. He is one of my new "forever friends." We stopped for prosecco before going to my apartment to unload the luggage. I loved introducing Quay to all of my new friends and showing off our beautiful Cortona.

My other introduction to Quay was prosecco while in Rome and it (as I knew it would) only took her a day to fall in love with it. On the second day in Rome, at exactly six (daily prosecco time), she said looking at her watch, "Isn't it prosecco time?" Since that day, always at six she asked me the same question for her entire visit, "prosecco time?"

We had dinner at the Brazilian restaurant with Mara and during that dinner along came my lurking friend. Mara, in her fiery Italian, told him to leave me alone and if he even walked by the restaurant while I was dining there she would have him hauled off by the *poliza*! She could do that too, her partner is a Cortona *polizia*!

After dinner it was off to the Fusion Bar, a visit with Massimo and talking of our plans to visit Perugia the following day. Angiolo, sweet, sweet man said not to worry about the bus not running on Sunday morning, he would be taking us to the train station in Terontala. *Ciao, ciao . . . domani mattina* at nine sharp for cappuccino.

Arriving at my apartment, we found that the key would not open my door; try as we did, nothing worked. We went back to Mara's seeking her partner (another Alessandro) the *polizia*, me asking if he had a gun and could blow my door open. He followed us home, the key still failing to open the door; with brute force, he kicked open my door (thankfully, without breaking it). What a sexy kick, I like the *polizia!*

The next morning we decided no luggage, we were taking clean socks and undies, a toothbrush, light traveling, just our style. An idea we could have had no idea how fortunate we would be to have made this decision until a few hours later . . . oh my!

At the train station we were disappointed to find that on Sunday only a late afternoon train would be going to Perugia, but Angiolo once again saved the day.

"*Andiamo*, I will drive you there!"

He drove us to the train station in Perugia. On the way we decided to take the train from Perugia to Assisi so Quay could visit S. Francesco of Assisi and have lunch and we could take a train or bus back to Perugia. Smooth sailing in Assisi and we were back in Perugia by three. The entire train station was packed with people, it spilled out to the piazza, crowding the bus and taxi lines. It was maddening. When Angiolo had dropped us off he mentioned there was a futbol game but how many people could fit into the stadium, not this crowd!

I waited in line for a taxi and Quay in line for bus tickets . . . forever! I was able to flag a cab but he told me taxis were not permitted up to "town center" because of the Chocolate Fiesta. The what? I thought it a ball game; no, "*Grande Fiesta!*"

We finally got tickets to the mid point up the hill (it is a mountain) but that was as far as the buses were allowed to go. Jumping off of the bus, I told Quay, "No problem, there is a sky people mover all the way to the top." Wrong; it was shut down except for people leaving the city.

We were forced to walk up the entire mountain to our hotel. Please . . . kill us now, it would be less painful. Had we had the luggage we had in Orvieto it would have been left at the bottom of that mountain. When we checked into the hotel, he asked about our luggage and we just laughed!

Perugia was chocolate everything and a party was going on. Masses and masses of people, it looked like Mardi Gras in New Orleans at midnight. It was much too crowded for us. The next morning we shopped and ate and off to Cortona! Home sweet Home!

We had a great time in Cortona, seeing the sites, meeting all of my friends and showing Quay what eating at its best is all about. Fresh vegetables, no chemicals, no injections in the animals, no sulfates in the wine, the freshest olive oil in the world, and those wines! I even talked Quay into going home, hiring a gardener to plant and tend to a great garden, fresh vegetables, no chemicals; I can't live on store bought veggies when I return!

We hated to leave Cortona but it was time to go to Florence, the beautiful city of art and Michelangelo and teaching Quay of the Medici family. The train and taxi ride were great, no problems but the rain had set in and we were hungry. Food, now that's a thought, an expensive one in Florence. We were use to sharing vast amounts of food, *vino della casa* (lots) and only paying small prices, about 13euros each. Not in Florence, a small shared lunch with one glass of wine each for the dear cost of 69 euros about $80 and that was for just a lunch, not a wonderful feast like we enjoyed in the hilltop towns.

Dinner was less (much less) than remarkable at the same outrageous prices and shopping with Ponte Vecchio and all of the designer shoppes was made easy, and expensive. At one small boutique, in the window was a fabulous leather coat. It was red, in the finest soft leather, like butter and reversed into a plush suede.

The owner was standing on the sidewalk smoking with another *uomo* and I asked, *"Quanto costa?"*

"650 *euros*," he replied and I told him I may be back. He then told me to bring my husband back and I let him know I wasn't married and the male chauvinist pig had the audacity to tell me that was why I didn't buy the coat! Hold me back, Quay, because I am going to punch his lights out. Get me out of Florence!

The next day we were off to Pisa, Quay's last night before returning to her life in Coppell. It rained the entire time but we still had fun and we were missing one another before she left and counting on the next time we would visit. Quay was returning home and I was off to find Pinocchio!

Forever Friends: spirit-lifting, joy-bringing, gift-giving, love-sending, heart-mending, problem solving, laughter-sharing, soul-searching, story-telling, fun-seeking . . . forever friends!

# Finding Pinocchio

Pinocchio is Italian, originated in Italy. Is Pinocchio a marionette, a boy, a fairytale, a town . . . a town in Italy? I didn't know but I did know I was off to find Pinocchio.

The original title of the book, *Le avventure di Pinocchio*, written by Carlo Lorenzini (1826–90), pen name Carlo Collodi, and the first chapter of *La storia di un burattino* (as it was called) appeared in the July 7, 1881, issue of a weekly paper for children.

*The Adventures of Pinocchio* were serialized in the paper in 1881–82 and published in 1883. The first English version was published in 1892 and in 1940 the Walt Disney cartoon ensured that the character of Pinocchio would remain familiar.

*The Adventures of Pinocchio* is a book I read to my children, my grandmother read to me and my children have read to their children. It is a great fun read and while I live in Italy it was as important to find the place of origination as was the Chocolate Factory in Perugia. I am not sure but I strongly believe the movie with Johnny Depp, *Charlie and the Chocolate Factory*, is based on the Chocolate Factory in Perugia.

In *Firenze* (Florence) it reminds you in countless ways, through sales at all venders of every conceivable toy or Christmas decoration or other various trinkets, that Pinocchio is nearby and not to be forgotten. While in *Firenze*, I inquired as to where Pinoccio originated from (in Italy), if there was a town, a factory or other places of history celebrating Pinocchio. Some said they thought there was a factory between *Firenze* and Pisa, there could be a town named Pinocchio but no one could tell me where and no one I met had ever visited.

I left *Firenze* and headed for Pisa in search for this elusive Pinocchio. Quay and I walked in the rain through Pisa, her shopping and me seeking Pinocchio to no avail. She bought Pinocchio trinkets and I came no closer in my search.

I saw Quay off at the Pisa airport the next day and I was off to find Pinocchio. I went to the train station and asked where I might find

Pinocchio; the ticket agent looked at me with a wry smile (I think she thought me a bit crazy) but she was kind and said she thought I might find Pinocchio in Lucca. That's all I needed, I was off to Lucca.

While traveling to Lucca, I thought it might be a good idea to find a book about Pinocchio and the book may give me a clue or clues to finding this thing called Pinocchio.

When I reached Lucca, I immediately found a book store but no books on Pinocchio. I once again starting asking, "Where oh where could this Pinocchio be?"

An ancient old man, about the tenth person I asked, told me he thought Pinocchio was in a town called Collodi. Collodi is a small town, not far from Lucca, a short bus ride. I was not anxious to go there, thinking surely this could not be the town of Pinocchio, would the town not be name Pinocchio? What is in the name Collodi, and where is Pinocchio?

Following my need to know, not my heart, I got on the bus to Collodi continuing my search. There were few people on the bus, all Italians going home from Lucca getting off at various stops along the way. I ask the lady next to me but she said she spoke no English and did not seem to want to chat in my Italian. I was left on my own but that did not stop me; I was going to find Pinocchio!

Collodi, of course, now it made perfect sense; that was his pen name. Collodi is the tiny village in Tuscany where his mother was born. I knew that now I was going to find Pinocchio!

I was joyous getting off of that bus knowing I had finally gotten to the right place and I was at last finding Pinocchio. Collodi is a small village with streets too steep and narrow for cars and must be explored on foot.

Lying just below the town is Villa Garzoni. Carlo Lorenzini (Carlo Collodi) was born in Florence but his uncle was custodian of the Villa Garzoni and he often stayed there as a child. Just on the other side of the road from the Villa is Pinocchio Park, a theme park for children based on Picnocchio's adventures; I had found Pinocchio.

Since my visit to Collodi, I now own two books in English, one

*Pinocchio* translated by E. Harden, and the second book *The Adventures of Pinocchio* translated by Carol Della Chiesa. While both books are the same, there are some differences in translation causing me to read and re-read both books, comparing the differences. It is still a fun read, and it was great fun finding Pinocchio!

# Cioccolato Caldo

*Cioccolato Caldo* or hot chocolate as we Americans know it has always been my winter favorite drink. When I moved to Cortona it was late spring, way past the time for *cioccolato caldo* but all of the bars still had posters up advertising. The posters show a cup filled with *cioccolato caldo* with a spoon standing up in the middle of the cup. It did not look appetizing to me, very thick and very dark chocolate. In the states we have milk and cocoa not something thick and so dark.

When Quay and I went to Perugia, the annual Chocolate Factory festival was in progress. I had never seen so many different types of chocolate. They had dessert chocolates, stress reliever chocolate, sleepytime chocolates, sexy chocolates and every other type imaginable. I, being the shopper, I wanted one box with an assortment of all of their different types of chocolates. The girl told me I would need a wheel barrel to take it with me and therefore what I wanted did not exist. They had so many different chocolates labeled for hot chocolate it peaked my interest on what this *cioccolato caldo* might taste like.

The Italians never over indulge, not in food or drink. They have certain times to have foods and what they drink even have specific times. Processco, only one, is for early evening, port is always for after dinner and hot chocolate is a winter early evening drink and they never have more than one cup.

American's, well, we definitely over-indulge on everything. Give us something we like and we will eat it or drink it until we can hold no more. That is the way we are with our foods, our processco, wine and how I eventually became with cioccolato caldo.

By the time Quay returned to the states, the Italians said it was now the right time to drink *cioccolato caldo*. That night, Angiolo asked me to meet him at il Bar Sport, one of our favorite afternoon hangouts, at six for my first experience in drinking hot chocolate "the Italian way." He ordered for both of us and after about ten minutes two steaming cups of this wicked brew were delivered to our table with the spoon standing in the middle of the cup. Also delivered was a steaming small pot of cream. I asked Angiolo what the cream was for and he told me to ignore it, it was for American's that had not learned the pleasure of drinking real hot chocolate and they needed to add milk. I then asked if I needed to add sugar and was told just a small amount but I might want to taste it first. It was very hot and I had to wait several minutes before tasting, all of the time thinking I was not going to like this cup of dark and thick stuff. It looked as though they had just melted a candy bar and named it hot chocolate.

My first taste was like something I had never experienced. Delicious, beyond my wildest dreams! Oh my goodness, this was the best stuff I had ever drank, I was even willing to give up my processco for *cioccolato caldo.*

It did not take me long to finish that first cup and want another. When I suggested to Angiolo we have another cup, he said, "No, that is not how we do it in Italy, we never have more than one cup." I could not wait to bid Angiolo goodbye so I could go to another *il bar* and enjoy another cup.

I found excuses every day to not be with people, sneaking off in the morning, early afternoon and early evening for *cioccolato caldo.* I never had it at the same 'il bar' more than once a day for fear someone would find out I had more than one *cioccolato* per day. I was a junkie on hot chocolate until I realized I was gaining weight rapidly. Only one hot chocolate per day for me from now on!

# Artists of Cortona
## *'artist eye'*

I have traveled so many places in the world: Sante Fe, New Orleans, New York, San Francisco, Rome, Florence and many other places with piazza artists. I never spent much time looking at the art but I always enjoyed watching the artists; some very good and some just cranking out fast works for the tourist, much too commercial for me.

Living in Cortona was the first time I have ever had the time, or taken the time to meet and understand the artist. I love art, art work and the artist. I have dabbled in many of the mediums myself but I realized early on I did not have that "artist's eye"; I never have been able to see what true artists see.

Early on in my life, I went to Paris to study art, thinking I was a good artist. I was only in Paris for several months before I realized, compared to the serious artists who had studied the masters for years, I was nothing. I found I could not sit at the Louvre with hundreds of other artists and draw, sketch or paint. Instead I found myself just sitting there watching the other "true" artists. I thought for many years of my life that I would grow up to be a great artist, my dream died before my eighteenth birthday; I was never going to be an artist.

The University of Georgia has an art school in Cortona so there are many budding artists. Tuscany draws many artists from all over the world with its natural landscapes, historical buildings and medieval towns; no matter where you are in Tuscany you can sit for hours and paint or draw many different scenes without changing where you are sitting.

Walking inside and outside of the walls of Cortona, I would always see people just sitting or that is what I thought they were doing. It took me some time to slow down and realize that these people aren't just sitting, they are painting or drawing. The first time it dawned on me was seeing an elderly lady, sitting on the rock wall overlooking the valley. I was in my "let's photograph the people" stage and as I zeroed in on her with my camera, I could see she had a paint brush in her hand and a pad on her lap. Instantly curious, I walked closer to her and, yes, she had a palate with various colors, a paint covered jar with water and she was painting the landscape of the valley. I sat and watched her for two hours in which time she completed four different landscapes in watercolor. It was amazing to watch and added something else to my life in Cortona. Now I wanted to follow the artists and watch them paint.

After my discovery that people were not just sitting, I started looking everywhere for these artists. And they were everywhere: on the pataire, sitting on the stone walls all around town, in the *poppy* fields and the sunflower fields, on balconies throughout the town and some even on the sidewalks. I questioned how I had been here for so many months and not realized what they were doing, creating beautiful artwork.

I wanted to know these artists, what inspired them, and why Cortona made them want to paint but mostly, I wanted to fined that "artist's eye" I wanted to see what they saw.

My experiences with the artist were incredible. One artist taught me to draw a self-portrait from a mirror. It was one of my best experiences. She is an English artist and lives in the hills of Cortona eight months of the year creating her art work and four months at her gallery in London, selling her creations. She and her husband met twenty years ago while on separate vacations in Venice; they fell in love and returned a year later to marry in Venice. They are both artists and like me found Cortona by accident and made this there home and a new life together with their beloved art. They have a great life.

Another artist friend of mine thought it would be educational for me to sit behind her while she painted and watch as she created her art. This is exactly how I found my 'artist's eye.' Wherever we sat, I saw the big things, the simple things, the overall. If we were on the balcony above the *immobiliario's* office, overlooking the main piazza, I saw buildings and people. But not Jennie; Jennie saw the details, the water running down the front of the building, the time on the clock of the tower, the dents in the bell tower, the old man sleeping on the park bench and even the dog peeing on the steps. Jennie has that "artist's eye." I never saw these things until she brought them alive on the canvas through her watercolors. This happened no matter where we went; she always saw things that I didn't even know were there and that is how she gave me the "artist's eye." Now, no matter where I go, or what I am doing, I stop and look and see what is really there.

When I talk to my artist friends about what inspires them, they all say everything. They are inspired by everything they see because they have trained themselves to see much more than we normally see, they stop and truly look at the beauty of our world and they create that on canvas.

Kandis was so inspired by the fig tree outside of her kitchen window that she did an incredibly beautiful study of fig trees. Not just the tree, the details of the leaves, the branches; she can see the whole tree all of the way to its very roots. Another study she did was of little blue birds. She had a bird fly onto her shoulder staying with her in her studio for days inspiring her. It is that incredible "artist's eye" that makes a true artist. Now that I have the "artist's eye," can I be an artist too?

# Moth Balls

Leaving Café La Saletta, after my *pasta con crema*, I thought for a moment that Piazza Repubblica was on fire and smoke was filling Via Nazionale but no there was no fire, no smoke; it was *nebbia* (fog). *Nebbia* is like living inside of a cloud, dense and damp.

Nothing I have ever experienced. The clouds you walk through for just a moment in Hawaii or the mountains of Colorado just tip the imagination of the *nebbia* of Tuscany.

I had been through the sheets of rain, the grape picking and now I was to enjoy the *nebbia* knowing as the *nebbia* rolled out of Tuscany the true cold of Tuscany would be blowing in. The fields have been plowed and the new seeding had taken place; we were now waiting for the olives to be picked and pressed.

The tourist had left for the season and we were donning winter wear. We had on undershirts, a button-down shirt, and a pullover sweater and for most, a woolen jacket and always the scarf. I was with my new down winter coat from Enzo's store and I think the only one in town already wearing gloves. The Italians don't think it is cold yet, just fresco.

With the wearing of wool, I had been noticing the tiniest of holes in some jackets, scarves and sweaters. I had no clue as to what caused these holes, perhaps just wear and tear. Drinking my cappuccino this morning, with the bar full and all of the tables crowded with high school students and others going to work, I detected an odor I had not thought of in thirty years. Moth balls! Yuck!

Growing up, the most important person in my life was my grandmother. She was full of life and full of love. The safest place in the world was up in her lap, lying against her ample breast with her arms around me. I associate many scents, aromas and smells to my grandmother. Gardenia, the slightest hint, was her perfume, she taught me never to wear it but to walk through it for just that subtle, soft elusive, almost non-existent scent, keep them guessing, she always said. Baby powder, she covered me in it after ever nightly bath. Fried chicken, homemade breads, pies baking in the oven and the Sunday roast with potatoes, onions and carrots. Cedar, everything she owned was in a cedar closet or cedar chest. And then those terrible moth balls . . . they make me ill!

I swore at age eight that I would never own, use or smell a moth ball when I grew up. I have managed to steer clear of them until now, living in Cortona.

Okay, so I realized I was in a world where people used moth balls, an ancient habit that had not yet died in Cortona, but that did not mean I had to use them. Moths don't really eat your clothes, right? I was not buying or using any moth balls.

I returned home to prepare for a party I was attending that evening. My clothes had been on my suspended clothesline for three days now. Even though the rains had left us, what with the cold and now the *nebbia,* clothes could not, would not dry. I iron many of my clothes dry but they have to be almost dry before the ironing works. I checked the line but no, they were still too wet to iron.

I would have to rethink what I was going to wear. I opened my armoire and started looking over what few clothes I had left. I had two pair of pants on the line, one dirty and two clean pair along with three sweaters and two button-down shirts. I had socks and scarves that were clean and plenty of panties and undershirts.

I took out a pair of black wool pants, a red sweater and matching scarf. This would be a nice look for tonight. As I was about to hang them over the chair I noticed a tiny little hole in the sweater. A hole in my sweater! No, there were three holes in my sweater and two in my pants and many in my scarf. On *mio Dio*, the moths have attached my few remaining clothes. Not moth balls, please!

Now I think there is a true conspiracy in Cortona: the Italian men undress you with their eyes, the lack of dryer and the temperatures and *nebbia* make it impossible for your clothes to dry and what you have left are eaten by moths. I truly will be naked in Cortona in the winter!

# Let's Cook

I think I have finally, after all of these months, visited every restaurant in Cortona. I have learned all of the names on the menus, chosen my favorite dishes in each restaurant and learned not to eat the tripe. I made myself taste the tripe because it is one of the specialties, but that does not mean I have to like it or for that matter, ever try it again.

I have acquired trade secrets from some of these wonderful restaurants . . . recipes! I learned many of the restaurants in Cortona and in Tuscany use recipes from a famous cookbook readily available in most of the stores and shoppes in Cortona; this great book is *Flavors of Tuscany* and has become my bible of recipes from Tuscany. The restaurants and the cookbooks have taught me to put chicken livers in my ragu and Bechamel in my lasagna.

I do love the olive oils and visiting the olive fields, picking and watching the olives being pressed has almost made me an expert. I can tell just by the color if it is excellent oil, and the aroma gives me the fullness of the body of flavor I know I will taste. I have learned how to bottle, store, cook and eat the olive oil. Olive oil is the liquid gold of Tuscany.

The olive picking begins in November and continues into December but never later than December 13, Santa Lucia's day. The picking is still done by hand, not to bruise the olives. The olive trees are from the Etruscan times, over 2,000 years ago, and the oils are known as some of the finest in the world.

Picking was amazing to watch, as the olives are shaken from the trees onto a net and hand-picked. The pressing must take place within 24 hours of being picked. The olives are washed, and then crushed between large stone wheels into a paste. The oil is then extracted from the paste using a centrifuge and filtered to remove impurities.

The *prima spremitura* (first pressing) produces extra-virgin oil, the highest quality. The oil in the remaining paste is extracted chemically and is of inferior quality. The *prima spremitura* can be found in the stores in Tuscany in December and in the States in January.

Buy small quantities of new oil and store it in a cool place (not in the refrigerator). The color of newly pressed oil is a limpid golden green. Olive oil is graded according to the amount of oleic acid it contains. By Italian law, extra virgin oil must contain less the 1 percent acidity.

Extra virgin oil is the basic fat used in Tuscan cuisine. Uncooked, it is used to dress salads, to preserve vegetables and fish, and to enliven a wide range of vegetable and antipasti dishes. Heated, it forms the basis of pasta sauces, stews, braised meats, roasts and many cakes. It is also used for deep-frying *patate fritte*!

I would have to write a cook book to share all of the foods I love in Tuscany. I am including some recipes that are easy, with ingredients available and seasonings we are all familiar with, adding some new twist to our basic thoughts of Italian cuisine.

First let's talk Lasagna, forget all of that cheese please, and use fresh pasta. Italians use little cheese in lasagna, opting instead for the wonderful flavor of *Bechamel*. Layer the pasta, *béchamel* and meat sauce, sprinkle parmesan on top and bake.

T=tablespoon

t=teaspoon

salt and pepper to taste

EVOO=extra virgin olive oil

### Béchamel

4 T butter

4 T flour–all-purpose

2 C boiling milk

Fresh grated nutmeg

Salt

Melt the butter in a small heavy-bottomed pan over low heat. Stir in the flour and cook, stirring continuously, for 1–2 minutes. Pour in a little of the milk and stir well. Gradually add all the milk, stirring continuously so that no lumps form. Cook over low heat, stirring all the time, for about 5 minutes. Season with nutmeg and salt to taste.

### Rich Meat Sauce

2 Cloves garlic,finely chopped
1 med carrot, finely chopped
1 med onion, finely chopped
1 stalk celery, finely chopped
2 T finely chopped parsley
½ C diced pancetta
4 T EV olive oil
8 oz veal or beef
4 oz chicken breast
4 oz chicken livers
1 oz porcini mushrooms, soaked in warm water for 20 min., then finely chopped
½ C dry red wine
2 C chopped fresh or canned tomatoes
Salt and freshly ground black pepper

In a large heavy-bottomed saucepan, sauté the garlic, carrot, onion, celery, parsley, and pancetta in the oil over medium heat until the onion turns light gold. Add the veal or beef, chicken breast, and livers and cook for 5–7 minutes more, stirring all the time. Add the mushrooms and cook for 5 minutes more. Pour in the wine and cook until evaporated. Add the tomatoes, season with salt and pepper, partially cover and simmer over low heat for at least 2 hours. The longer the sauce cooks, the tastier it will be, so don't be afraid of simmering for 3 or 4 hours. Add a little hot stock or water if it becomes too dry.

### Meat Stock

2 ½ lbs. of various cuts of beef with bones, neck, short ribs, etc.

2 carrots

2 onions

1 celery stalk

2 ripe tomatoes

2 cloves of garlic

2 sprigs of parsley

1 bay leaf

2 quarts of cold water

Put the meat, vegetables, and herbs into a large pot with the water. Cover and bring to the boil over medium heat. Season with salt and pepper. Partially cover, and simmer over low heat for 3 hours. Turn off heat and set aside to cool. When the broth is cool, remove the vegetables and herbs, and skim off and discard the fat that will have formed on top.

### Crostini all'aretina

### Sausage toast

1 C highly flavored fresh Italian sausages

7 oz. fresh stracchino (crescenza) cheese or a coarsely grated semi-hard stracchino cheese

Freshly ground black pepper

1 long loaf firm-textured white bread cut in half 1/2/1cm thick slices and toasted in the over

Squeeze the sausage meat out of the sausage skins into a mixing bowl. Add the cheese and pepper and mix very thoroughly with a fork. Spread each toast with a generous helping of the sausage and cheese mixture and transfer to a large, shallow ovenproof dish. Bake in a pre-heated oven 400° for 5 minutes, or until the cheese has melted and the topping is bubbling. Serve pipeing hot straight from the oven.

### Ribollita (soup)

3 cherry tomatoes (pricked with a fork)

1 lb. fresh white cannelloni beans or 1 ¼ cups dried cannelloni beans

2 cloves garlic

6 leaves fresh sage

Salt and ground black pepper

1 ½ T finely chopped parsley

Small sprig of fresh thyme

1 onion, thinly sliced

1 leek, thinly sliced

2 med. Carrots, diced

8 oz. Swiss chard, shredded

½ sm. Savoy cabbage, shredded

1 C chopped tomatoes

French beans

Peas

Zucchini

7 T EV olive oil

1 qt. beef stock

10 oz. firm textured white or brown bread sliced in half inch slices

Place the tomatoes in a large, heavy-bottomed saucepan with the beans, garlic, and sage. Cover with cold water. If using fresh beans, add salt to taste at this point. Bring slowly to a boil, cover and simmer for about 25 minutes for fresh beans or about 1 hour for dried beans. If using dried beans, add salt when they are almost cooked. Discard the garlic and sage and puree half the beans in a food processor or food mill. Put the parsley, thyme, onion, leek, carrots, Swiss chard, cabbage, tomatoes, and other vegetables in a large, heavy-bottomed saucepan with 4 T of oil over a moderate heat and sauté for a few minutes, stirring continuously. Add the pureed beans and the whole beans, followed by about two-thirds of the stock. Taste for salt. Cover and simmer gently for about 1 ½ hours, adding more stock if the soup becomes too thick. Heat a heavy-bottomed saucepan and add a ladle or two of the soup and a slice of bread. Keep adding more soup and bread until finished. Drizzle with 3 T of oil and sprinkle with pepper. Cover and leave to stand for 2–3 hours. Return to the heat and bring slowly to a boil. Simmer very gently for 20 minutes with stirring. Alternatively, reheat the soup in the oven at 400 for about 10 minutes. This soup is equally good served hot, warm, or even cold, depending on the season. Traditionally it is served in small, round terracotta bowls with little handles on either side. Drizzle a little olive oil into the bottom or each, then ladle in the soup.

### Gnocchi di polenta

2 qts. Water
1 heaped tablespoon coarse sea salt
3 1/3 C yellow coarse-grained cornmeal
4 T butter
1 quantity Meat sauce
1 ¼ freshly grated parmesan cheese

Prepare the meat sauce (your favorite). Bring the water to a boil with the salt in a large, heavy-bottomed saucepan. Sprinkle in the cornmeal while stirring continuously with a long-handled wooden spoon to prevent lumps forming. Continue stirring while cooking for 40 minutes. Just before removing from the heat, stir the butter into the polenta, which should be very thick, smooth, and soft in texture. Using a T, make oval dumplings, dipping the spoon in cold water to prevent the polenta sticking. Don't worry if the dumplings look rather untidy. Place a layer of dumplings in a fairly deep, heated ovenproof dish, spoon some meat sauce over the top, and cover with another layer of polenta dumplings. Continue in this way, finishing with a layer of meat sauce. Sprinkle with the cheese and bake in a preheated oven at 400 for 5–8 minutes, or until the topping is golden brown. Serve immediately.

### Paparo all'arancia

1 oven-ready duck, weighing 2 ½ lbs.

2 cloves garlic

1 sprig of rosemary

Salt and freshly ground black pepper

3 oranges (organic: not treated with any fungicide)

5 T EV olive oil

1 onion, coarsely chopped

1 carrot, coarsely chopped

1 stalk selery, coarsely chopped

½ C dry white wine

½ C sugar

1 ½ T water

1 T lemon juice

Wash and dry the duck and place the garlic, rosemary, salt, pepper, and the zest of 1 orange into the cavity. Pour half the oil into a large roasting pan. . Add the duck and sprinkle with ore pepper. Arrange the onion, carrot, and celery around the duck and drizzle with the remaining oil. Roast in a preheated oven at 375° for about 1 ½ hours. Ten minutes into the roasting time, pour the wine over the duck. Meanwhile, peel the zest off the remaining 2 oranges and cut it into very thin strips. Place in a small saucepan with cold water, bring to a boil, and drain. Repeat the process twice to remove bitterness. In a small, nonstick saucepan, heat the sugar, water, and lemon juice over a moderate heat until the sugar melts and caramelizes to a pale golden brown. Add the zest strips, stir over a low heat for 2 minutes, and set aside. Thirty minutes into the roasting time, squeeze the juice from 2 oranges over the duck. When the duck is done (test by inserting a sharp knife into the thigh if the juices run clear the duck is well done), remove the garlic, rosemary, and orange zest from the cavity. Transfer the duck to a casserole with the cooking juices and vegetables and spoon the caramelized orange zest over the top. Place over a moderate heat for 5 minutes, turning the duck once or twice. Serve hot.

## Agnello al forno
### Tuscan roast lamb
2 lb leg or shoulder of lamb
3 cloves garlic, each sliced into three
1 T chopped rosemary
½ C white wine vinegar
Salt and freshly ground black pepper
½ C EV olive oil

Using a small, pointed knife, make deep slits in meat and push a garlic slice and some rosemary into each incision. . Mix the vinegar with, salt, pepper, remaining rosemary, and oil in a large deep bowl and add the meat. Leave to stand for two hours turning the meat in the marinade. Preheat the oven to 200°. Place the meat in roasting pan, pour the marinade over the top, on the meat and roast for about 1 hr (depending on whether the lamb is to be pale pink in the center or well done), basting at intervals.

## Fegato alla salvia
### Calf's liver with sage
1 ¼ lb calf's liver, thinly sliced
½ C all-purpose/plain flour
4 T EV olive oil
3 clove garlic
6 leaves fresh sage
Salt and freshly ground black pepper

Lightly flour liver, shaking off any excess. . Heat the oil with the garlic and sage over a moderate heat in a large nonstick skillet. . When oil starts to sizzle around the garlic, raise the heat to moderately high. Add the liver and cook quickly to ensure tenderness, turning once. Sprinkle with a little salt and pepper when well browned and remove from the heat. Serve at once.

## Pollo ai semi di finocchio
### chicken with fennel seed

3 ½ lb a young oven-ready roasting chicken

½ C pancetta

2 cloves garlic, finely chopped

1 heaped teaspoon finely chopped sage

1 heaped teaspoon finely chopped rosemary

1 T finelychopped parsley

1 level teaspoon fennel seeds

5 T EV olive oil

Salt and freshly ground black pepper

Wash the chicken inside and out and dry with paper towels. Mix the pancetta, garlic, herbs, and fennel seed with a good pinch of salt and pepper and place in cavity.Use a trussing needle and thread to sew up the opening. . Pour half of the olive oil into a roasting pan and add the chicken. Drizzle with the remaining oil and sprinkle with salt and pepper. Roast about 1 hour in a preheated 350° oven, or until the juices run clear when a knife is inserted deep into the thigh. Serve hot.

## Fiori di zucca fritti—
### fried zucchini flowers

You may need your own garden for this as I have suggested for Quay—A high quality store may have zucchini flowers—*no lo so* (I don't know)

14 fresh zucchini flowers—taken before the zucchini has ripened

2/3 C all-purpose/plain flour

½ t salt

1 T EV olive oil
1–2 T cold water

Remove the pistil (the bright yellow center) and calyx (the green leaflets at the base) from each flower. Wash quickly and gently pat dry with paper towels. Sift the flour into a mizing bowl and make a well in the center. Add the salt and 1 tablespoon each of oil and water. Gradually mix into the flour, adding enough extra water to make a batter with a thick pouring consistency that will cling to the flowers. Heat the oil in a large skillet until very hot. Dip the flowers in the batter and fry until golden brown on both sides. Drain on paper towel. Fry all the flowers in the same way. Serve immediately.

Enjoy!

# Are We Who We Are
## Or
## Are We Where We Are

All of my life I have said: good morning, how are you and good night, never thinking about what I was saying, that's just what came out. That is no longer true. Now I say *buon giorno, come va, buona sera* and *buona notte*; everything comes out in Italian first.

All of my conversations are started in Italian switching to English only if I am stumbling over a thought or speaking to someone who does not know Italian. The language I hear in the mornings upon waking and the last language I hear before going to bed is Italian. My habits, my ways, my dress and my customs are becoming more Italian, and I am losing more every day of my American ways. It shows in the foods I eat, the things I drink and the daily routine I so religiously follow. I am looking and acting more Italian. Italians visiting even ask me in Italian for directions or the perfect place to eat, just assuming I am Italian. It makes me wonder if you put me in a convent would I be a nun, if you put me in an opium den would I be a drug addict?

Are we who we are or are we where we are?

I have surely fallen in love with Italy. I love the foods of Italy, of Tuscany. Just yesterday Donna (Donatella) called saying she had just gotten fresh sausage from the farmer down the way and asked me to dinner. I told her I would gather up what I had and we would feast.

Donna is one of the "Goddesses of Cortona," finding peace here after her husband had passed away. She came to Cortona on vacation with a friend, fell in love and decided to make this her home. She was visiting with Lorenzo *(immobiliario)* in Piazza della Repubblica inquiring about a place to rent. Lorenzo told her of several apartments in her price range in town. She told him, "No, I want to be way up on the mountain and be able to see the entire valley."

He said, "Not on your budget, just not possible."

She said that she had angels on her shoulders and it would happen.

Enzo came upon the conversation saying he had a house at the top for rent. She made her offer to him and he accepted. He told Lorenzo he would pay him a commission but Lorenzo said, "No way, she has angels."

Donna's house is indeed at the very top; a walk I hate to make and only have in fact walked up twice. She will come get me in her car, drive me up and even walks me most of the way down. I love the walk down, especially at night. It is a beautiful steep walk and if you lost your footing you would roll, twist and turn all the way to the center and bottom of Cortona. The narrow lanes are invitingly lit at night and I find myself wanting to share the walk with everyone.

When I come down late at night, all lights in the houses dark. I want to shout out and tell them to wake up and see how beautiful these lanes are. Last night I told her I would walk up. The night was so clear, I just wanted to be outside. I ran down to buy a loaf of fresh bread; on my way back, I stopped at the garden next to Chiesa S. Niccolò and picked up two tomatoes, a long zucchini and three carrots. Back at my apartment I put the chestnuts my neighbor had given me in the bag and added some figs.

On the walk up I noticed some pears had fallen off a tree in a yard I passed. I did not want them to ruin so I took four of them and added them to my bag. The pears here are like everything else, so sweet and delicious. I even love the juices dripping onto my chin.

We were in for a great dinner and the only thing we had to buy was a loaf of bread for about fifty cents.

Donna cooked the sausage and I sautéed garlic and carrots in fresh olive oil, then added the tomatoes and zucchini and a pinch of rock salt. We roasted more garlic and olive oil for our bread. Everything was from the garden. No chemicals, no hormone injections in the cows in Italy. The wild boar sausage is homemade by the farmer's wife with herbs from her garden. The fruits picked right off the tree, or just under. Show me a place I could have foods this fresh and this good!

We have wicker-shrouded demijohn's we take to a local farmer and have filled with red wine. Donna keeps two of these jars at her house but I only have one. A glass of wine bought this way works out to about twenty-five cents.

I wanted roasted chestnuts and when Donna asked if I knew how to roast them. I said, "Of course, on a cookie sheet in the oven for some undetermined amount of time with the oven on or about 350." I did not have a clue what I was talking about but with the wine we had both consumed, it all sounded perfectly correct, just like I was following a recipe. I popped them in the oven and we were off to the living room with our wine, pears and figs to watch a movie.

We drank more wine, got into the movie and forgot all about the chestnuts. But the chestnuts did not forget about us. A bomb went off in the kitchen; not a bomb actually, it was bombs, many, many, many bombs! I ran into the kitchen, opened the oven door and missiles starting shooting out at me with great force. Holy gods, what have I done? I just wanted roasted chestnuts. Later, I found out that you must pry the shell with a knife just enough to let the air out before roasting them.

I was full, ready for bed and that lovely walk to my house. Donna wanted the exercise after our meal and walked down with me. On our way down she was sharing with me that there was nothing in the world she was afraid of, bragging about it! We both feel brave moving to Italy alone and love to do a bit of boasting. About that time a cat chasing a mouse (tiny little mouse) ran out in front of us and Donna literally jumped in my arms. So much for being afraid of nothing Donna!

# Gubbio

It had been cold and wintry for months; the tourists were gone, the days were short and the nights were long. The population had fallen from 6,000 to 1,500 almost overnight and our American friends had long ago departed leaving only us die hards in Cortona.

But we still loved it, the nights were full with the biggest brightest moon I had ever seen (yes, it does scream "a big pizza pie and that's amore!") The cold was crisp with winter fires burning, fine wines and great foods keeping us all warm and happy.

There were three of us American girls, Kandis (the artist), Donna (the widow) and me having breakfast and making plans for our day. There was a slow drizzling rain but the temperature was the best we had seen for a while and left us needing adventure. I was the first to say let's go on a day trip, let's go to Gubbio! We didn't have a map but I sort of knew where it was, somewhere amid the slopes of Monte Ingino in Umbria at the Appenine foothills. Only a mere suggestion of adventure and we were off in Donna's car, rain slicked streets, no map but we were thrill seekers and looking forward to fun and excitement.

Gubbio was a town that I had read so much about but had never seen a picture of and only imagined it would be much like the other hilltop towns of Tuscany and Umbria that I had visited. To my surprise coming into to the town of Gubbio, I was instantly disappointed. The town appeared to be flat with a main road running straight through. A town much like Camucia. Was I remembering the wrong town, had I read it wrong, was this not a hilltop town with Monte Ingino, Monte Calvo and Monte San Girolamo rising behind? And what about the cable railway that takes visitors to the top for that most amazing view?

The first saving grace for the town was me spotting the ruins which I knew had to be The Roman Theatre dating from the first and second centuries of the Christian era. Yes, it is in ruins but intact enough to let you feel and imagine what it was like so many years before. I jumped out of the car, my umbrella shielding me from the rain, walked the theatre, and sat on the stone steps and let my mind go all the way back to the Roman Times. Imagination is a great thing and I always find myself lost in that space.

Kandis and Donna awoke me from my great fantasy and we were off to find the rest of the town. It was market day in Gubbio and not a parking place to be found. Driving almost to the end of this flat town we found a big parking lot serving a major housing complex and felt lucky to find it.

We found an archway into the walled city of Gubbio, still unimpressed, seeing only the backsides of low slung buildings; we continued walking down stone steps on narrow lanes between the buildings. Three blocks of walking down these steep stone steps brought us to the main street of Gubbio. Much to my surprise, the street was filled with shops, boutiques and eateries, the architecture and stone streets were beautiful. We had finally found the true Gubbio, or so I thought.

We stopped at the nearest bar for espresso and a sandwich and to get our bearings. We were told to follow the main road to the end, enter the door beside the church, walk the tunnel in the building until we came to the elevator. On the elevator we questioned where we were going and what a surprise we found, the real Gubbio.

We exited into a Piazza; at the Palazzo dei Consoli where they have the race of the Ceri, a religious feast celebrated May 15, the anniversary of the death of the patron saint, Ubaldo. The streets were filled with artisans' shops of locale ceramics, paintings and other crafts. This is what I thought Gubbio was going to be, filled with monuments and ancient landmarks, we had arrived!

But had we really arrived, no, not yet. The best was yet to come. We walked into another building with the same tunnel like structure, thinking it was the same building and elevator that brought us here but no, it was another altogether different building, another tunnel and another elevator. We stepped into the elevator rising quickly, feeling like we were going up for miles, the elevator stopped and we were at the top, the peak of Gubbio.

We exited at the Basilica of St. Ubaldo, from here you could see what I now refer to as "the hidden" hilltop town of Gubbio. The view was spectacular and from here I could see the Rope-Railway Station, cable cars that take you along the mountainside for a view of the world.

When visiting hilltop towns in Italy, do not leave out Gubbio. Gubbio is known to be one of the most medieval and historical towns of Umbria.

# Dancing in Montepulciano

Italians love to dance; they are good dancers and will go for miles to dance. In Cortona there are not any places the Italians refer to as a "dance hall." We do have restaurants and clubs with music and many with live music on the weekends but no dance halls.

The closest place for great music and dancing is Montepulciano about a forty-five minute drive from Cortona. The dance clubs do not open until nine so it is perfect to have dinner in Cortona or any of the surrounding towns and then make the drive to Montepulciano.

I love music and I love to dance and most of my friends are the same way. Hanging out with Angiolo was always fun and we had talked for months about going dancing but just never got around to going. Enzo and Donna met Angiolo and me for dinner one night and we started talking about dancing which led into making plans to go the following weekend.

Angiolo always dresses nice but I had not seen him dressed up, I mean really dressed up; but that Saturday night he was dressed to kill. I guess this was a big thing to him or he really wanted to impress me because he went all out with a perfectly cut suit, silk ascot and shoes so shiny I could see myself.

Donna went all out as well and I guess, so did I. We went shopping a few days before, had our hair done and our nails done and we looked pretty great! Nuccio at my salon saw me before I met with Angiolo, he called Angiolo and told him how beautiful I looked and he better catch up with me before someone else swept me away.

The four of us met at La Saletta for a glass of prosecco before going to Camucia for dinner. Enzo was as cute as I had ever seen him and I was almost jealous that he was not my date but I do adore Angiolo.

Enzo was sitting across the table from me at dinner, he put his fork down, looked at me and said, "Carlotta, you look like you are about 25 tonight."

I said, "Thank you and I think I love you." I must have been look-ing good too!

After dinner and wine, Enzo drove us to the dance hall for a fun night of dancing. When you enter the dance halls in Italy you are given a ticket which gets stamp every time you order a drink which is totaled up when you leave so take plenty of money as the bill can get big fast.

I had always heard that Italian men were always flirting and in many cases pinching women. They do flirt, they do believe in "amore" but I have never been pinched. Not in Tuscany but maybe in Rome. The one thing Italians never do is flirt with a woman who has an Italian boyfriend or someone they perceive to be a boyfriend.

Once Angiolo and I starting hanging out together all of the time, everyone just assumed we were dating as in boyfriend and girlfriend and my dating Italians came to a screeching halt. The men just assumed we were romantically involved and that was that, but I was still having great fun and did not mind.

The dance halls are a totally different world, the men and women don't care if you came with someone, if you are sitting with someone or even if you are dancing with someone. If they want to dance with you they just come and take you by the hand and off to the dance floor you go.

Many times I was on the dance floor dancing with Angiolo and a guy would just come up and start dancing with me. Trust me, rules do not apply. I know this is not done to be rude, I think it is just the way things are when dancing in Italy. Great fun!

# Make me Feel Beautiful

Giovanni had a late tour in another town and I did not have a date. Amy and I felt this would be a Saturday night to have great fun together. Amy took the bus up to the Piazza and I met her there at seven. We had a great one hour walk on the partaire and stopped along the way for espresso. We then went to the Fusion Bar for our nightly prosecco on the sidewalk so we could also visit with friends as they strolled by many stopping for a drink and a longer chat.

For many years Amy has taught English at the University in Arezzo. She tutors children at home but teaches adults at the University. One of her students, Alessandro, and his girlfriend stopped by and Amy introduced me as her aunt. Even though Alessandro has taken two years of English he still does not speak it well and much prefers his native Italian. He spoke really fast and I was only picking up part of the conversation. He was so to die for handsome, the typical magazine cover Italian man with long dark curly hair, six feet tall, strong jaw line and beautiful eyes. Made me wish I was thirty again. Amy and I went on to Dardano's for dinner and then back to the piazza for coffee and waited for Giovanni to join us at midnight.

The next day Amy sent me an e-mail, read like this:

> Dear Carlotta,
> This is what my student Alessandro wrote about you:
> Tua zia e' proprio una bella donna, sembra piu europea che americana, ha dei lineamenti molto eleganti.
> Translation: "Your aunt is really a beautiful woman, she seems more European than American, and she has very elegant features."
> I'm so jealous! XOXOXO, Amy
> Make me feel beautiful!

# I Made Ragù for Italians
## And they Loved it!

No country I have ever visited or lived in celebrates life like the Italians do. Life itself is a celebration, every meal is a feast and every occasion amounts to a festival. But all things in Italy, celebrations, festivals, rituals or traditions all center around food. Food is the mainstay of the Italian livelihood and with that food, the wine and the cheer and the good times.

Americans grow up seeing (in movies on the big screen) the heavyset Italian women in the kitchens appearing to be cooking all of the time, apron tied around ample waist with a soup spoon in hand and a smile on her face, a long table, a large family consisting of generations. That's the mental picture I always had of the typical Italian family and I was sure it was so.

But the true picture is really very different; the women are not heavy set, the families (immediate) are much smaller today, many only having one or two children and not just the women cook. The men are fantastic cooks, taught by their mothers. The tradition of all those wonderful foods live on. The tables are long and full of generations of family, some attending the feast are not really family but taken in by the families and thus becoming family. That's me, that is where I fit in, I just melded into those beautiful families, learning new tastes, new foods (intestines-Trippa alla fiorentina)- no thank you! I think, I will pass, nope, not an option! We must all try all of the foods and learn the techniques of making these traditional Italian dishes.

I had enjoyed all the restaurants of Cortona, eaten in many of the homes, learned to love the taste of many new foods, learned to say no to ones I had tried and not liked and now it was time for a dinner in my honor. My friends, Italians, English and American, wanted to throw a dinner party for me. Two things were required of me for this dinner party: the first, I had to choose the menu and secondly, I had to participate, meaning I had to cook at least one signature dish. Oh my, me cooking for an Italian, could they ever enjoy my cooking, these the best cooks of the world, and, of course, I had to make something Italian!

Everyone was joining in, in paying for the foods, in preparation of the foods or in bringing prosecco or wines or desserts for this grand feast we were planning. Coming up with the menu was my first hurdle, it had to include a food I could cook and not be laughed at and enjoyed by all. That meant it had to be something in Italian that I knew how to make, not just how to make, it could not be an American version of an Italian food, it had to be traditional and Italian. I started going over list of simple Italian foods that I ate all of the time, that I loved and that others would love as well.

Some of my favorites, simple foods consisted of roasted duck, Italian sausage, *verdura, insalata mista*, pasta and ragù and *bruschetta*. I often ate (two or three times a week) at a La Pizzeria at the end of my street. I found this restaurant during my first week in Cortona, known for it's pizza but the sausage was offered to me on my first visit and it was love at first bite. My meals at La Pizzeria always, after that first time, consisted of sausage, *spinai, verdura* with lots of extra virgin olive oil, *patate fritte* and half a liter of *vino rosso*. It did not matter that I spoke no Italian and the owners spoke no English, they knew me quickly and my dishes always magically appeared before me. So at this, sausage was first on the list. Another of my favorite trattoria in Cortona is Trattoria Dardano, known for their roasted meats and pastas with many different sauces but their ragù being my favorite. I love the roasted duck and ate it every chance I got along with a large plate of pasta with Ragù. I thought we or I could in no way compete with Dardano's roasted duck so that was not going to be on the menu but I came up with the idea that maybe, just maybe I could make a Ragù, pleasing the palates of my Italian friends.

Now, with the thought of ragù being my signature dish, I started thinking about my ragù experiences while living in Cortona. My first experience was at a Pizzeria and Pasta family restaurant in Camucia. The first time I had their ragù my mouth, taste buds were hit with a flavor that at first I could not recognize but knew it was something

I never experienced in a ragù of any type. I rolled it around in my mouth, a nice flavor, funny texture but I could not identify what I was eating. I stuck my fork in another piece, and placed it in my mouth by itself, no pasta and ah ha, it was liver. Not just any liver, it was chicken liver. I said to Angiolo that I thought they had mistakenly put chicken liver in my ragù. He said no, it was not a mistake that is one of the main ingredients of ragu. Chicken liver, who could imagine and now I can't imagine a proper ragù without chicken liver.

I was definitely on to something, I would make ragù and I would make it with chicken livers. Even knowing this, I knew I would still need a recipe to pull this off. That meant visiting my friendly chefs at all of my favorite restaurants, the mamma at Molesini Mercato and comparing all of that with the Flavors of Tuscany cookbook. The shopping for our dinner went well, breads from the locale bakery, vegetables from the *green grocier*, meats from the locale butcher, prosecco and wine from Molesini Enoteca, fresh pasta from the pasta shop and everything else from Molesini Mercado.

Yes, you're right, it is not easy shopping like in America, everything at one big supermarket but the Italian way is indeed the best way. Everything is fresh, just picked, just butchered, just baked and the fresh pasta comes right off the pasta machine while you wait.

Buying the prosecco was funny; when I asked how many bottles I would need for a party of twenty, he ask me if it was for Italians or for Americans. When I told him most were Italians, he said I would need half as many bottles as I would normally buy for the same number of American's. Are Americans known for over doing?

The other great things about the Italian families are the way they prepare their foods. First in the villas or *grande casas* they have three ovens. The conventional is the kitchen oven, the outside oven which is very large allowing you to cook entire pigs or whole wild boar, and let's not forget the fireplace. Their fireplaces were built large and deep, this is where they often roast their meats, in this case our sausage, and make the *bruschetta*. Tasks were divvied up; Angiolo, Donna and I would shoppe, I would make the ragù, Angiolo would prepare the sausage (in the fireplace), Kandis would be in charge of the salad, Enzo would make the pasta and help Angiolo with the bruchetta, everyone else would bring wines, ports and desserts.

I had visited and read everything I could find about a proper ragù, had my shopping list and was ready to tackle feeding my Italian friends. My job of making the ragù had to be done the day before to allow for the hours of cooking it required. Mamma Molesini had me confident that I would make a great ragù and I was ready. Angiolo, who lives with his mamma and papà, has never cooked in his life but let me know he was available to be my kitchen assistant. He chopped and diced while I browned meats, cut up and cooked my chicken livers and prepared my tomatoes. We were a great team and on to making the best ragù ever!

On the night of the dinner, it was fasinating to watch the fire crackle as the juices popped from the sausages and I was intrigued by the guys rubbing the bread with fresh garlic and adding olive oil before toasting our *bruschetta* on the open flames of the fireplace.

But I have to say, the best part of the dinner was my ragù! I made ragù for the Italians and the Italians loved it! Angiolo even went home and bragged to his mamma that his American Lady friend made the best ragù he had ever eaten. I am sure mamma loved hearing that!

# Baby Giulia Elisa Arrives

Giovanni and Amy, and everyone else had been awaiting the arrival of baby Giulia for months. She was nine days over-due and we were all trying to be patient.

I received the phone call from Amy on Wednesday, June 7, at 8:00 am, with Amy excitedly telling me she thought she was in labor and could I come with her and Giovanni to the hospital? I was so excited and full of questions but thought it best to wait until I was face to face with Amy.

"Giovanni is on a tour in Cortona but can pick you up when he is finished. Can you come?"

"Yes, of course I can come. I will call Giovanni and find out where and when he can pick me up. Will you be okay until we get there?"

"Of course, I'm not even really sure I am in labor, just some pains and I want to go to the hospital and let them examine me."

"Okay sweetie. See you soon. Bye"

I called Giovanni and we arranged for him to pick me up at the end of my street in an hour. I called Amy back to make sure she was alright. She was ironing and said she would be fine.

When Giovanni and I arrived, Amy was cleaning the bathroom, the bidet and said she wanted to cut the roses in the garden before we went to the hospital.

"Enough is enough Amy. *Basta, basta* . . . let's get going," said Giovanni. Amy was still not ready but moved it right along when she discovered she was bleeding.

The new hospital in Camucia does not deliver babies. The expectant mothers have to choose between Arezzo, Casteglion del Lago or Siena. Arezzo was out for Amy, she did not like the hospital. Casteglion del Lago was out for Giovanni as his baby had to be born in Tuscany not in Umbria. That left the hospital in Siena. A forty-five minute drive from Camucia.

Amy's doctor was at the hospital when we arrived. After examining her, we were told that she was not in labor yet but would be staying at the hospital.

The doctor came to the hallway where I was waiting and, thinking I was the mother of Giovanni, told me it would be late Thursday or even Friday before the baby would arrive. It was nice to know we had a couple of days to get things in order.

The hospital has a wonderful birthing apartment but only one and it is first come, first serve. Amy was lucky. The apartment was not in use and it was assigned to us. Two bedrooms, a kitchen and a spa bath much like a nice hotel suite. We set things up in the apartment and had a nice lunch together. Giovanni was going to take me back to Cortona and he was off to finish up things at work and get things together for a long hospital stay. I would come back Thursday morning and stay with them until the baby arrived.

I was in my apartment, like an expectant grandmother just biding my time. Looking back over the last year and remembering all of my new experiences helped me pass the time. I called Amy about every hour to make sure she was doing well.

This is my second June in Cortona and it amazes me the time could fly by so fast. My first June in Cortona was so hot it sent me to the mountains. This June is so cold, I have had to borrow sweaters, scarves and pashmenas to stay warm.

I decided months ago to make my next new home in Portugal and would be leaving June 18 to meet an agent in Portugal and view possible homes for me. I was looking forward to the next stage of my life but I knew I was going to miss all of my new friends in Cortona.

At nine my cell phone rang and it was Giovanni telling me that Amy was already in labor. I was so disappointed that I would not be there for the birth. I stayed up very late waiting for the phone call telling me she had arrived. I fell asleep at some point and woke to the shrill of my phone. Baby Giulia had arrived safely at 7:02 Thursday morning. A big baby at nine pounds one ounce and twenty-one and a half inches long.

I looked forward to spending my last week in Cortona with Amy and the baby.

# A. L. Jones

My favorite place in Cortona, where I can enjoy peace and quiet, a good book and good food is La Pizzeria on Via Dardano. I always sit at a four top corner table where I can see everyone in the front room. I always order *salsiccie, verdura* and a half liter of *vino rosso*. Sometimes I add *patate fritte* or *spinaci* but I always have the *salsiccie*.

Having so many friends and so many things to do in Cortona my quiet side needs the solo time about once a week. La Pizzeria is where I always come for that solitude, usually for lunch but sometimes I come for dinner and sit on the back patio.

People watching is another one of my favorite pastimes. This is a great place to listen to the tourists talk about Cortona and Italy. I also enjoy the Italian families who come together to share a pizza for lunch. La Pizzeria has a homey feel and the locals love the pizza served here and they love the family who owns the restaurant.

When I first started coming here, I spoke very little Italian and had a hard time with the menu but after only a few visits the family knew me and my favorite foods would begin to appear. We found a way of communicating and they helped me along learning the language. I often come here with my friends and always bring people visiting me from the States.

As I sat at my corner table on a Wednesday afternoon I noticed another lone diner at the opposite corner of the room. She too seemed to be seeking some alone time and enjoying a book. She noticed me watching her and sent a nod my way. No words where spoken on this day. We only shared that nod of recognition and went back to ordering our food and reading our books. I remembered seeing her in town before and it was obvious she was no stranger to Cortona. She seemed very comfortable here and I began to wonder about her. I wondered if she lived here fulltime, if she was an American, a tourist or a local.

She appeared to be American but not having heard her speak, I wasn't altogether sure. I was so curious about her that I left my table to go to the bathroom, having to pass her table. I was able to take a fast glance at her book. The book was in English. She must be American. Maybe she is English but I don't think so.

More times than not, when I came to La Pizzeria for my lone time, this lady that held my curiosity would be there too. For weeks we never spoke, it was just that nod that let us each know that we acknowledged one another. My curiosity was killing me and I vowed that the very next time I would introduce myself.

One week later, that time finally came. We were both in the restaurant, sitting across the room at our appointed tables. I had just finished my lunch when she came into the pizzeria. Now was my chance to meet her.

I walked up to her table, "Hello. My name is Charlotte and I can't help but notice you dine here as often as I do."

"Yes, she replied, I have noticed you many times. My name is A.L.Jones and I am pleased to make your acquaintance. I just love this place for the quite and to take a break from all of the people. You know we are in the busy tourist season and it is nice to sneak away and enjoy a good book."

"Do you live here?" I asked A.L..

"Sometimes I live here and you?"

"I am going to live here for a year and decide what to do after that."

The owner came to take A.L.'s order so I felt I should leave. I bid A.L. goodbye and walked out even more curious about this lady and her circumstances.

I continued seeing her week after week but we never spoke again. The heat in Corona was unbearable and I left to visit the Dolomites for a couple of weeks. When I returned I continued to see A.L. on and off until one day I realized I had not seen her for a while.

I tried to look back, to remember how long it had been since I had seen A.L. but my memory failed me and I thought maybe it had been since the end of August or maybe even the middle of September. It felt funny not having her in the restaurant and I was sorry I had not gotten to know her. Obviously, she did not live in Cortona.

Now it is June of the following year. I am once again seated at the four top table in the corner, reading my book. I look up and A.L. is walking in the door. I am so delighted to see her again and this time I am going to really meet her and get to know her.

I waved and said "A.L., it is so good to see you again. Remember we met last year?"

"Yes, of course I remember. You love to read and you love your time here."

"A.L., this year, I would really like to get to know you. Do you think we can spend some time together? I am leaving this month but would really like to visit with you before I go."

"Well, let's make sure we get together before you depart. Enjoy your lunch."

That was it. That was all I got in the way of conversation from A.L.

The next to my last day in Cortona, Vivienne and I were having lunch on the patio of La Pizzeria, saying our goodbyes and reminiscing about our time together. We paid our bill and walked into the front room and there was A.L.. I asked A.L. if I could join her for a while and said goodbye to Vivienne.

"A.L., I have always been so curious about you. I am curious by nature and want to know why people make their home in Cortona. I have gathered information on everyone else living here but you remain a mystery to me."

She laughed that great laugh that I had become accustomed to hearing and said, "Mystery, I am no mystery!"

"Oh, but you are to me. Please tell me about yourself."

"Well, I am A. L. Jones and I am from rural Illinois, from corn, soybean Illinois. What else would you like to know?"

"Well, everything! What do you do in Cortona? How long have you been coming here? When and how did you find Cortona and why?"

Before I share her story let me describe A. L. Jones. She is timeless and she is ageless. She wears her hair short with a mixture of brown and grey. Her hair has never been touched with dye nor has her face ever been decorated with make up. She is generally dressed in trousers, buttoned down collared shirts with the shirttail out, the most sensible shoes and sometimes even a fisherman's hat.

Ms. A. L. Jones is the most comfortable woman in her own skin, in her own being that I have ever met. She is what I would love to be. She is adventurous, daring, intelligent and secure. She doesn't hide behind designer clothes, a made up face or a false air of being. She is remarkable.

A.L. began telling me her story. "I am a professor at a State University and have always been of a curious mind. I have read since I was a young girl and marveled at what life could be. I live by two codes. One from when I was a young girl, 'It is my fault if I am bored if I have a good book to read' and as I grew into a woman, 'Just because we have to do it alone is no reason not to do it!' My parents raised me to believe I could do or be anything in the world. They gave me the time, the freedom and the love to achieve."

"A.L., when did you come to Cortona?"

"That's a long story. Thirty-five years ago, just after the Turkey/Cypress war, the head of the Archeology Department at the University received a grant for an archeology dig in Cypress. I wanted to go. I had no credentials. My degree was not in Archeology nor had I ever studied in that field. But, I wanted to go. The head of the department was a friend and on that basis alone, I decided to apply.

"When I met with the head, he said 'A.L., you have no credentials. How can I accept your application? What am I to base my decision on?'

"I had thought long and hard before the interview and had come up with a bit of a can spill about my education, not yet receiving my tenure, my other experiences, my love and admiration for archeology . . . etc. But when he asked the question my mind went blank. Who was I kidding, I had no credentials. Regaining my senses, I looked at him and stated, in a very matter-of–fact tone, 'well sir, you will be on an island, and everyone will want to swim. Do you want to bare the responsibility of a drowning? I, on the other hand can help you. I am a certified life guard! I can go as your appointed life guard.'

"He fell over in great laughter." After composing himself, he looked at me, dead in the eyes and said 'Okay, A.L., you can come with us.'

"I fell in love with the digs and started going every year. Twenty-three years ago I came on a dig to Siena. While in Siena, I read about the Etruscan Period, and the Etruscan Tombs in Cortona. I knew it was a place I wanted to visit. I left the group and headed for Cortona.

"When I arrived in Cortona . . . was there only one hotel? I'm not sure but there were no vacancies as it was the tourist season. I went to the tourist office to inquire about someplace to stay and they said that I might try at the Instituto and gave me the address. I asked directions and took off for the Instituto.

"On my way, with darkness approaching, wondering what was the Instituto, thinking perhaps it was a bordello but willing to stay anywhere for one night. Reaching the Instituto and reading the welcome sign 'The Convent' stay with the nuns. Laughing and relieved, I entered the building and my 'one night' has turned into every year, for the summer, now going on my twenty-third year. I hope to have many years of returning every summer to Cortona . . . my home away from home!"

# Ciao Cortona

I had it all wrong; my thinking was not right and it took me months to realize the meaning of my "new" life. I thought I came to Cortona to run from a broken heart and to delay the memory of my mother passing. I did think I was broken-hearted and I did think missing my mom would be too much to bear but I did not know I needed to forgive them and in forgiving them, I would find I would also thank them. I was no longer a wife, waiting on the sidelines to see where my life was going, in what direction my husband was going to take my life, our lives. I wasn't even aware that I could and should be part of the decision in making those life plans; I was just along for the ride, his ride, not mine. I found I was no longer the adult waiting to become the caretaker for the elderly, aging parent, just waiting to take on the role I expected to take on in my life.

If someone had a need, I was there to fill that need when all of the while I was filling up space and time, my space and my time but not with my life, only with a life born and re-born by the needs of others. Who am I? What am I? What do I want to be? Those are the questions that really found there way with me in Cortona.

When I look back on the time that sent me as a traveler to Cortona, it was like my mother and husband came together with the idea of freeing their butterfly, of giving me my wings and encouraging my flight, giving me once again the gift of life, now to be my life. I could imagine them saying, "If butterflies were meant to fly, then fly on little wing, our love is with you!" Thank you and you will always be with me. I boarded that plane with the spread of the big silver wings taking me across the ocean to that new world, that exciting new life and my new home in Cortona, Italy. Cortona, Italy is like no other place in the world for me, it is only here that I think I could find my new life and learn the many important lessons of that life. No longer do I think about what people have to justify who they are.

No, now I see that person, not what that person has or what that person does, I really see the person: their morals, character and the love they share in their lives. Why did it take this wonderfully enchanting, noble town of Cortona, in the midst of all the medieval towns with their historic monuments, early traditions of feasts and traditions to bring me to my knees, to open my eyes, to thank others for what I am becoming and to learn what life is about and what my importance in this life is about? I've only just begun this adventure, this journey, this . . .my new life!"

My travel experience while living in Cortona have been the best of travel as I learned to take the time to enjoy the places I visited, to experience the festivals, the traditions, the foods and to get to know the people of the towns I visited. Never once did I leave a town that I had not met at least one, often many people of the town or village, that made a difference in my life, in the way I viewed their city or came away with a better understanding of their traditions and, of course, my palate always grew with the rich taste of their local foods.

My appreciation grew in leaps and bounds of the local farmers, craftsmen, artisans and yes, the shoemakers; these are places where family businesses, the arts, the crafts continue on, not year after year but decade after decade. My heart is in Tuscany and in Umbria, but my heart lives and grows in the most perfect place, my Eden, Cortona. Finding Cortona was simply an accident, the best accident of my life. I did not know Cortona, I had not heard of the book nor had I seen the movie *Under the Tuscan Sun*, I just got to Cortona by accident and fell in love and now Cortona will always be a place where I hang my hat and will always call home for some parts of each year. In finding Cortona, I found the people of Cortona and those are the people who taught me about life, love and things remembered.

One of my first encounters was of a man who did not speak English, had not traveled the world, had always lived in Cortona and worked in Florence and he has over these many months become one of the most important people of my life. His name is Angiolo and his love is Cortona and he holds my heart and my love as one of the best friends I shall ever have and I am so fortunate for him being a part of my life.

When I first met Angiolo he was preparing for his retirement and wondering where his adventures in life would now take him, being a simple man not requiring much yet fully happy with his life. He was looking forward to hanging out with his friends, doing volunteer work and enjoying his family: mamma, papà and a married brother with two children. Angiolo had always lived at home with his mamma and papà making him, as he says and as the Italians say, a *mammone,* a mama's boy.

Little did he know that some wonderful life plan would throw me into the mix of his world with him becoming my sidekick and him becoming my mentor, my teacher of the language and him being the forever historian educating me in Italian ways and customs. But thrown together we were and our friendship began to grow and come together as none ever has for me. Angiolo made my introduction into Cortona and Tuscany easy, taught me the history, traveled with me through the beautiful medieval towns and made my living in Cortona the best it could be.

I will miss my breakfast at La Saletta and the brother and sister team that always took care of me, Maurizio and Barbara Menci and their parents, and Bar Banchelli with Barbara, Beatrice and Cristina waiting on me as if I were family.

I will always have fond memories of sharing *cioccolato caldo* in the winter with Amy, Vivienne, Donna, Enzo and Angiolo, or those late night dinners and the dancing outside of Montepulciano.

My hair was an important concern of mine as I have bad hair and choose to wear it long. But I had no worries once I found Nuccio and in his shop was Sabrina the perfect solution to keep my hair looking good.

My groceries, shopping in Cortona with my living up hill, having no car was made easy by the Molesini family. The helped me make my lista in Italian, taught me how to make simple things and even went as far as delivering my groceries. Mamma Molesini taught me how to make ragù and papa Molesini took me hand in hand to Banca Popolare di Cortona and introduced me to Andrea and Stefano and told them not to charge me fees when transferring my money. I now always walk in the bank and tell them, remember I am not a tourist, I live in Cortona.

Shopping for clothes has been made easy by Enzo Accordi at his wonderful boutique; he always made sure he had my sizes in the latest Max Mara fashion. I was a walking advertisement for him in that beautiful grape colored winter coat.

My only true family in Tuscany, Amy and Giovanni and now baby Giulia. Giovanni known as the "best tour guide ever"; you can read it for yourself in all of the travel guides and Rick Steves' new book.

My favorite new friend who travels and lives part-time just outside of Cortona is John Michael Lerma a fellow author and chef, Cook Books and Culinary Tours in Italy. He has a newsletter and website, GardenCountry.info. When visiting Tuscany stay at his villa and enjoy his divine cooking classes and the meals!

Famiglia Cenci at the Trattoria Toscana made my mouth water with their foods of traditional Tuscany. I loved how they explain what is in each dish and how I might prepare the same at home. Vivienne and David the most beautiful couple in Cortona with hearts so big they even had room for me. Thank you for the shared wines, ports, prosecco and those dinners.

Roberto Ghezzi, my immobiliaro at I-CREA, you know I could not have lived here without you, finding me a place and answering all of my endless questions.

Giuliano, thank you for the most beautiful flowers, they are the way to a woman's heart and they are the only flowers ever delivered to my home while living in Cortona.

Ivan Botanici owner of Galleria "Il Pozzo," thank you for my painting, it hangs in the spotlight of my living room along with the two paintings from Jennie; these three paintings are my prized watercolors. Kandis, thank you for the wonderful oil of "The Worshipper" now hanging in my bedroom and the first thing I see upon waking every morning.

I am leaving out so many of the precious people who made me at home in Cortona but they know who they are and how I feel about them and will enjoy the comforts of the warm spaces in their hearts for years to come.

One person, not in Cortona but back home, that has come to mean the world to me is Molly. Molly, I could not have continued to write or even think about having my book published if not for you and your prayers. Your letter was the first and only letter I received from home by post, it made me cry and it made me warm and fuzzy. My grandest thanks are to you!

*Ciao, ciao Cortona . . . Ola Portugal!*

# Um Doce Vida in Portugal
## In The Beginning

I moved to Cortona, Italy a little over a year ago to start a new life. I was divorced, retired, the kids were grown and I had no aging parents to care for. It was, I found, to be the best time so far in my life.

Living in Tuscany proved to be a great experience and I all of a sudden had a new family. A large family, as I had met just about every person in Cortona. They had taken me in as though I was family. I found I was so in love with having new experiences and I did not want that to end in Cortona.

Europe is about my favorite place in the world. I have been traveling in Europe off and on for years. Many years ago I lived in France and in Germany. I knew I wanted the experiences of Cortona to expand to other places in Europe. Where, was the question?

I spent days thinking of all the wonderful places in Europe I had visited and what it would be like to live in one of those places. Then I remembered how awesome it was to move to Cortona not knowing anyone or for that matter, anything about Cortona. So, I decided I needed to move somewhere that I had never visited.

Once I made up my mind that it had to be a place I had never been to, the decision was easy. I was moving to Portugal. I ran out and bought maps and books on Portugal.

Not knowing anything about the country, other than where it is located, it was hard to think about what part of the country I wanted to live. It was so exciting laying the map across my bed, opening up a whole new world.

Water, I wanted to live near the water. In Cortona I was a two hour drive from either coast and I had missed the water. I figured out quickly that I did not want to live in northern Portugal, in the mountains. It left me with Lisbon (Lisboa) on the water, or the Algarves. The Algarve is a large region with many small towns along the coast. I was ready for a villa or an apartment in a villa with a swimming pool and a garden patio. I could picture it in my mind.

The Algarves won out. I no longer fancy big city life and there are so many small towns in the Algarves to choose from. According to the scale on my map it would take about an hour to drive from the west coast crossing the whole Algarve and arriving at the Spanish border. Along that drive is a town or village about every fifteen minutes. Now I just needed an estate agent to find me a property. I was off to the I-net bar to start exploring.

Searching the internet is when I found out that Portugal has its own language. Brazilians also speak Portuguese. I had always thought the Portuguese spoke Spanish. Now I am going to have to learn Portuguese! My friend in Cortona that owns the Brazilian restaurant is from Brazil. Maybe she will give me lessons.

# An Agent in Portugal

Finding an estate estate agent for the Algarves was easy. There are so many web-sites for vacation villas, apartments or shared living for the traveler. Most of the places are geared toward the two-week vacationer and I needed long term, maybe up to a year.

The English go to the Algarves to vacation all of the time so there was no language barrier for me to deal with, now it is just a matter of personal choice. I chose one because he offered taxi service from the airport in Lisbon. From my map it appeared to be about a two hour drive from the Algarves. I did not want to rent a car and drive.

I sent an e-mail and before I had finished my other work on the computer, he sent a reply. He asked all of the normal questions: when I was coming, how long I was staying, what was my budget and did I know the great differences in prices between "in season" and "out of season"?

After I answered all of his questions, he said he would research and in a day or two e-mail me properties to view. I had chosen my apartment in Italy from the internet and had no problem doing the same for Portugal.

It was March when this search for my home in Portugal began and by the first of June the agent and I had a bit of flirtation going on and he wanted to meet me. He said I could fly from Florence to Lisboa and take a train for three and a half hours to Fargo or I could fly to Sevilla, Spain catching another plane to Fargo where he would pick me up.

After checking with *agenzia di viaggi* (travel agency) in Cortona, I made arrangements to fly to Sevilla and on to Fargo. I did not realize until I got to the airport in Sevilla that I would be flying on a very small plane to Fargo or I would have gone to Lisboa.

It is June 3 and I will be leaving Cortona on June 18 to meet Andre' and look for a new home in Portugal. . I love his name and the e-mails he has been sending me. I have no idea of his age or what he looks like but he certainly writes pretty!

It felt like I was going on a blind date. I was so excited about meeting him. I worried what my reaction would be if he turned out to be a frog . . . or worse. I took a deep breath and thought if he was a frog he could still be a great agent and I was not going to Portugal to fall in love with a man. I was going to Portugal to fall in love with Portugal.

After my deep breathing and calming myself I had a worse thought. What if he thinks I'm a frog or worse? What if he turns out to be 20 and here I am 55 . . . oh my, have I lost my mind . . . whatever was I doing? I at least needed to know his age before embarking on this journey.

I e-mailed him and asked him to call me, saying I would love to hear his voice. Was I flirting? Yes, I was! He called immediately and I immediately fell in love with his voice, that accent . . . wow!

After a few minutes of talking to him I mustered the courage to ask his age . . . to my delight he is 53 . . . I can do 53! When he asked me, I thought about lying and saying 45 . . . I could pass for that (on a good day) but alas, I told him the truth. He replied, "Ah . . . I shall fall in love with an older woman."

I only realized after we hung up that I did not ask him if he was married. But surely he would not be this amorous if he were married. Would he?

I was on the plane from Sevilla to Fargo and day dreaming about Andre.' I was in the first seat and literally sprang out of it when the plane stopped on the tarmac. At the top of the stairs I saw him and he saw me. What a beautiful man, I almost could not move . . . I kept telling myself one foot in front of the other . . . now move! Our eyes held as I walked down and three steps from the bottom, I tripped.

Tripping and falling into his arms was a life changing experience. Could I fall in love? Was this the man of my dreams?

TATE PUBLISHING *& Enterprises*

Tate Publishing is committed to excellence in the publishing industry. Our staff of highly trained professionals, including editors, graphic designers, and marketing personnel, work together to produce the very finest books available. The company reflects the philosophy established by the founders, based on Psalms 68:11,

"THE LORD GAVE THE WORD AND GREAT WAS THE COMPANY
OF THOSE WHO PUBLISHED IT."

If you would like further information, please call
1.888.361.9473
or visit our website
www.tatepublishing.com

TATE PUBLISHING *& Enterprises*, LLC
127 E. Trade Center Terrace
Mustang, Oklahoma 73064 USA